Creating Your Own Growing Space:

A Step-By-Step Guide Towards Creating A Community Garden and Introduction to Land Ownership

Bryan McAskill

ISBN: 978-0-578-30716-9

Contents

Review

Starting a community garden can be an exhilarating experience; although a very arduous set of tasks to complete and run successfully. Throughout this guide, you will be presented with many tips and helpful information for how you can approach the process of starting your very own community garden. The information in this text is meant to help you begin creating your own growing space. You may take away some information to begin feel confident enough to have a few house plants that you will grow, or begin planning your backyard garden. But for those interested, you will be presented with a step-by-step guide on how to create your own community garden.

With more people adjusting to more natural lifestyles, which include growing their own foods, I have created this guide to help simplify the process and create a template that can be used to bring together members of the community and help to close the gap of food insecurity. This guide is written with the intent of teaching how to legally create a community garden space in your own community, while learning to generate a sustainable income for expansion and leverage for complete land ownership.

As the world has become more commercialized in regard to building for retail and real estate, much of the natural land we have has been torn down and reconstructed. Working within the confines of most cities and small towns who do not have nearby access to quality foods, there's a growing need to find creative, but sustainable ways to grow produce with initiatives such as community gardens, and opportunities for land ownership.

It is my hope that those who take the time to read this text will enhance their knowledge with growing plants, create plans to start a community garden (or get involved with an already existing one), and encourage readers to become mindful of the many land ownership opportunities that are currently available.

Let's begin!

1 What Is A Community Garden?

A community garden can be urban, suburban, or rural. It can grow flowers, vegetables—or community. It can be one community plot or many individual plots. It can be located at a school, hospital, or in a neighborhood. Whatever you decide to grow, I'd like to encourage you all to think about community gardens as "community-managed open spaces." These differ from a park or public space where some other entity ultimately decides the purpose of the site and maintains it. Community gardens are where the residents of a community are empowered to design, build, and maintain spaces in the community for the purpose of growing their own produce

Why Start a Community Garden?

- Combat food insecurity, both in quantity and quality.
- Build on the resources of cities, towns, and counties to deal with urban problems.
- Fight climate change by reducing the distance food travels, and minimize the carbon footprint of food.
- Boost the local economy.
- Improve community health through better nutrition and increased physical activity.
- Create social capital.
- Help build stronger and safer communities.

As we have begun to move closer/back towards a more sustainable, healthier, and plant-based lifestyle, many families living in the city,(particularly the inner cities) would like to grow their own fruits, vegetables, herbs, and flowers. The typical "food desert" has now become more of a prime location for potential regarding growing produce. Many communities have consistently been taken advantage of and not included in the development of infrastructure within their city. Developing a "green space" that is sustainable for residents, while using laws and local regulations, can help to maintain a positive and necessary addition to your local community.

Not everyone has access to a local farm or have space within the area of their home. Some want to save money on their food bills. Others like the freshness, flavor, and wholesomeness of home-grown produce. And for many, gardening is a relaxing way to exercise and enjoy being outdoors. There are also families from other cultures who would like to grow traditional foods from their home countries that are not always available in the supermarket. Community gardens beautify neighborhoods and help bring neighbors closer together. They have been proven as tools to reduce neighborhood crime – particularly when vacant, blighted lots are targeted for garden development. Community gardens provide safe, recreational green space in urban areas with little or no park land, and can contribute greatly to keeping urban air clean. Those who are lucky enough to have sunny backyards or balconies can plant a garden whenever they have the time and energy.

Steps Towards Starting Your Own Community Garden

1 Get Your Neighbors Involved

There is a lot of work involved in starting a new garden. Make sure you have several people who will help you. Over the years, my experience indicates that there should be at least ten interested families to create and sustain a garden project. Survey the residents of your neighborhood to see if they are interested and would participate. Hold monthly meetings of the interested group to develop and initiate plans, keep people posted on the garden's progress, and keep them involved in the process from day one. The surrounding neighborhood for where you intend to start a community garden, will need contributing members of that neighborhood to be involved for a variety of reasons. Most notably, residents will take care of a space if they live close by. Having gardeners who live in close proximity to the garden also helps with having someone being able to get to the garden in case of an emergency and/or get help from other relatives and friends who live in the area. You will need some eyes and ears on the garden when you're not there and having neighbors help with this crucial step is a great way to continue making progress with your community garden.

2 Form A Garden Club

A garden club is a way of formally organizing your new group. It helps you make decisions and divide-up the work effectively. It also ensures that everyone has a vested interest in the garden and can contribute to its design, development, and maintenance. A garden club can be formed at any time during the process of starting a community garden; however, it's wise to do so early on. This way, club members can share in the many tasks of establishing the new garden and provide access for members of the community to become involved easier and help provide input, gather information, and provide questions. If there is another garden close by or near your community it would be helpful to connect with them to help connect resources and connect with individuals who can help, as well as create interest for potential gardeners who wish to grow in another space. A garden club can be created before you even have an identified space if you have several committed members who plan to remain involved.

The typical garden club will have many functions, including but not limited to:

- Establishing garden rules
- Identifying land for garden and developing "blueprint" for space
- Accepting/reviewing garden applications

- Making plot assignments
- Collecting garden dues (if any)
- Paying water bills
- Resolving conflicts

***The typical garden club has at least two officers: a **President** and a **Treasurer**, although your garden club may have more if necessary. Elections for garden officers usually can be held annually.

3 Find Land For The Garden

Look around your neighborhood for a vacant lot that gets plenty of sun--at least six to eight hours each day. A garden site should be relatively flat (although slight slopes can be terraced). It should be relatively free of large pieces of concrete left behind from demolition of structures. Any rubble or debris should be manageable–that is, it can be removed by volunteers clearing the lot with trash bags, wheelbarrows, and pick-up trucks. Ideally, it should have a fence around it with a gate wide enough for a vehicle to enter. It is possible to work with a site that is paved with concrete or asphalt by building raised beds that sit on the surface or using containers. You can also remove the asphalt or concrete to create areas for gardens, but such a garden will be much more difficult, expensive, and time-consuming to start. A site without paving, and soil relatively free of trash and debris is best. The potential garden site should be within walking, or no more than a short drive from you and the neighbors who have expressed interest in participating. If the lot is not already being used, make sure the community supports establishing a garden there. It's best to select three potential sites in your neighborhood and write down their address and nearest cross streets. If you don't know the address of a vacant lot, get the addresses of the properties on both sides of the lot--this will give you the ability to make an educated guess on the address of the site. I suggest you identify at least three potential sites because one or more might not be available for you to use for various reasons, and you want to end up with at least one that works out.

4 Find Out Who Owns The Land

It is illegal to use land without obtaining the owner(s) permission. In order to obtain permission, you must first find out who owns the land. Take the information you have written down about the location of the sites in step 3 to your county's tax assessor's office. ***Your city's Tax Assessor's office will have this information.*** At this office, you will look through the map books to get the names and addresses of the owner of the sites you are interested in. If you are planning to use a park or playground area for your garden space, most like the city and local government you live in are the designated "owners" of the land space; you will have to reach out to your local Parks and Recreation Department to discuss plans and to gain approval.

5 Find Out If Your Proposed Site Has Water

While you are researching site ownership, contact the water service provider in your area to find out if your potential site(s) has/have an existing water meter to hookinto. Call your water provider's customer service department, and ask them to conduct a "site investigation". They will need the same location information that you took with you to the Tax Assessor's office. Existing access to water will make a critical difference in the expense of getting your project started. Depending on the size of your garden site, you will need a 1/2-inch to 1-inch water meter. If there has been water service to the site in the past, it is relatively inexpensive to get a new water meter installed (if one doesn't already exist). If there has never been water service to that site, it might cost much more for your water provider to install a lateral line from the street main to the site and install your new meter. You will want to connect to your local government to connect resources and save yourself costs of paying an independent water bill (more information will be provided on how to save rainwater later on within this guide).

6 Contact The Landowner

Once you have determined that your potential site is feasible, write a letter to the landowner asking for permission to use the property for a community garden. Be sure to mention to the landowner the value of the garden to the community and the fact the gardeners will be responsible for keeping the site clean and weed-free (this saves landowners from maintaining the site or paying city weed abatement fees). Establish a term for use of the site, and prepare and negotiate a lease. Typically, groups can lease garden sites from landowners for $1 per year. You should attempt to negotiate a lease for a least three years (or longer if the property owner is agreeable). Many landowners are worried about their liability for injuries that might occur at the garden. Therefore, you should include a simple "hold harmless" waiver in the lease and in gardener agreement forms. For more information on the lease, and the hold harmless waiver, see 8, "Signing a Lease". Be prepared to purchase liability insurance to protect further the property owner (and yourself) should an accident occur at the garden. For more information on the hold harmless waiver, and liability insurance, see 8, "Signing a Lease", and 9, "Obtaining Liability Insurance".

7 Get Your Soil Tested

It might be advisable to have the soil at the site tested for fertility pH and presence of heavy metals. Contact a private lab or be granted permission to test soil yourself by your local government officials. You can start by testing the pH (Potential Hydrogen) of the soil to determine if it is neutral, acidic, or alkaline. Anything 7 of above is alkaline (7 being neutral). If soil is acidic, this does not necessarily mean you cannot use the land. It will just signify that much more work has to be done which includes, tearing up several

layers of the ground, getting a large amount of soil from another location (which can be expensive), and regularly testing your soil months leading up to the official start of your community garden and/or any growing space.

In the picture above, you'll see a fairly neutral pH testing strip of about 7 which is adequate for growing your plants. You may purchase a standard pH testing strip online or at a store. It can be helpful to search for testing strips made specifically for testing soil.

You can find a few pH testing strips for gardens in the links below:

https://gardentutor.com/toolbox/ph/

https://www.amazon.com/Garden-Tutor-Strips-3-5-9-Range/dp/B07YZT5ZPJ

https://www.the-compost-gardener.com/soil-ph-test.html

Soil Texture Analysis

A simple method to estimate the percent of sand, silt, and clay, in the soil and determine its texture.

1. Get a quart jar from the supermarket with a lid or use any jar with a large mouth.

2. Fill the jar half full of soil

3. Wet the soil to a mud consistency and tap the jar to settle the soil.

4 Mark the level of soil on the jar with a marking pen or whiteout

5. If you have some Calgon put a teaspoon full in the jar

6. Add water to the top of the jar and shake the soil water mix until the soil is all mixed up in the water

7. Put the jar on a table and let the soil settle out for 40 seconds, mark the level of soil on the jar. This is sand portion in the soil.

8. Wait 6 hours and mark the level of the soil in the jar. The difference between the bottom mark, which is the sand, and the second markup is the silt portion of the soil. The total sand plus silt is the distance from the bottom of the jar to the second mark.

9. Calculate the percent sand, silt and clay by measuring the depth of the soil by measuring the distance from the bottom to the first mark up in inches which is the sand fraction, the distance from the first mark up to the second markup which is the silt fraction and the distance from the bottom to the third mark up from the bottom which is the sand plus silt plus clay fraction. Sometimes, when all the sand silt and clay has settled, the height of the soil is higher than when you marked the jar after making a mud solution. This can only be determined by letting the jar sit for several days. If you have the time to do this, then a more accurate calculation of % sand

silt and clay can be determined based on this new measured total height. Also, the percent sand, silt, and clay is a total volume percentage. The soil triangle and table below for soil classification is in percent by weight. You need to correct this problem by converting from percent volume to percent weight by multiplying the percentage of sand by 1.19, the percentage of silt by 0.87 and the percentage of clay by 0.94. These numbers are the weight ratios of bulk density compared to average bulk density of the material.

10. The percent sand is the depth of the sand divided by the depth of the total soil
11. The percent silt is the depth of the silt divided by the depth of the total soil
12. The percent clay is 100 minus the percent sand plus silt.
13. To determine the soil texture knowing percent sand silt and clay using the table below:

Soil Classification	Clay Soil	Loam Soil	Sandy Soil
Clay %	40-100%	7-27%	1-10%
Silt %	0-40%	28-50%	1-15%
Sand %	0-45%	23-52%	85-100%

14. A more precise determine of soil texture can be determine from percent sand silt and clay using the soil triangle (see picture below). This simple approach to determining texture will not work if the soil contains a lot of gypsum. Soils that contain a lot of gypsum are normally pinkish white in color and most likely would be avoided to begin with.

Soil Triangle

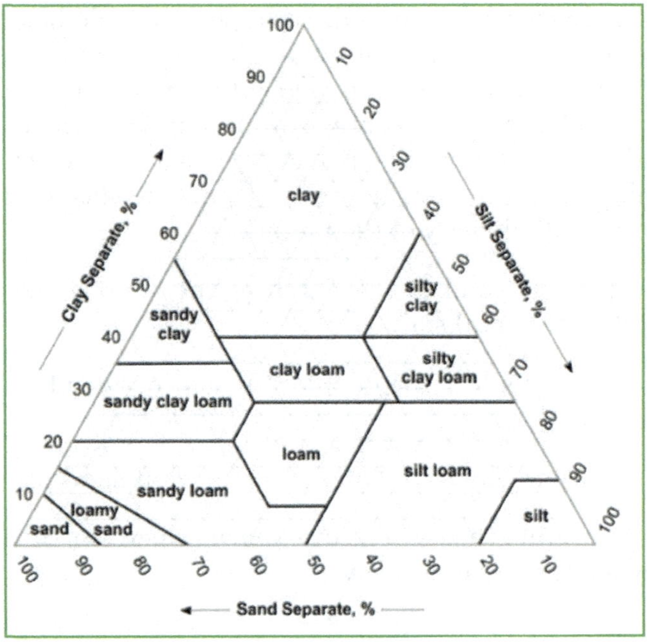

The Jar Test

Materials:

- Straight edged, clear jar
- Permanent marker
- Ruler
- Watch or stopwatch
- 1 tablespoon of powdered dishwashing detergent
- Mesh sieve or old colander

Procedure:

Jar filled a $^{1}/_{3}$ of the way full of soil.
Andrew Jeffers, ©2018, Clemson Extension

1. Using a mesh sieve or old colander, sift the soil to remove any debris, rocks, and large organic matter (leaves, sticks, roots, etc.).

2. Fill the jar $^{1}/_{3}$ full of the soil to be tested

Jar filled with water, leaving space at top.
Andrew "Drew" Jeffers, ©2018, Clemson Extension

3. Fill the remainder of the jar with clean water, but leave some space at the top.

Jar showing the coarse sand layer settled at the bottom of the jar.
Andrew "Drew" Jeffers, ©2018, Clemson Extension

4. Add 1 tablespoon of powdered dishwashing detergent

5. Cap the jar and shake vigorously until the soil turns into a uniform slurry.

6. Set on a level surface and time for one minute.

7. Place a mark the outside of the jar, showing the coarse sand layer settled at the bottom of the jar.

Jar showing the silt layer.
Andrew "Drew" Jeffers, ©2018, Clemson Extension

8. Leave the jar in a level spot for 2 hours.

9. Mark the top of the next settled layer with the permanent marker. This is the silt layer.

Jar showing the clay layer.
Andrew "Drew" Jeffers, ©2018, Clemson Extension

10. Leave the jar on a level spot for 48 hours.

11. Mark the top of the next settled layer with the permanent marker. This is the clay layer that has settled on top of the silt layer.

Using a ruler, measure and record the height of each layer, and the total height of all three layers.
Andrew "Drew" Jeffers, ©2018, Clemson Extension

12. Using a ruler, measure and record the height of each layer, and the total height of all three layers. Use the soil texture analysis worksheet below to record results.

1. The clay percentages are listed on the left side of the triangle. Lines corresponding to clay percentages extend from the percentages reading left to right (see red line).
2. The silt percentage is on the right side, with lines extending downwardly, diagonally right to left (see green line).

3. The sand percentage is on the right side, with lines extending upwardly, diagonally right to left (see blue line).

4. Track the lines with the percentages measured and find the spot on the triangle where all three lines intersect. The region where these lines intersect indicates the soil type present. The example shown represents a loam soil texture.

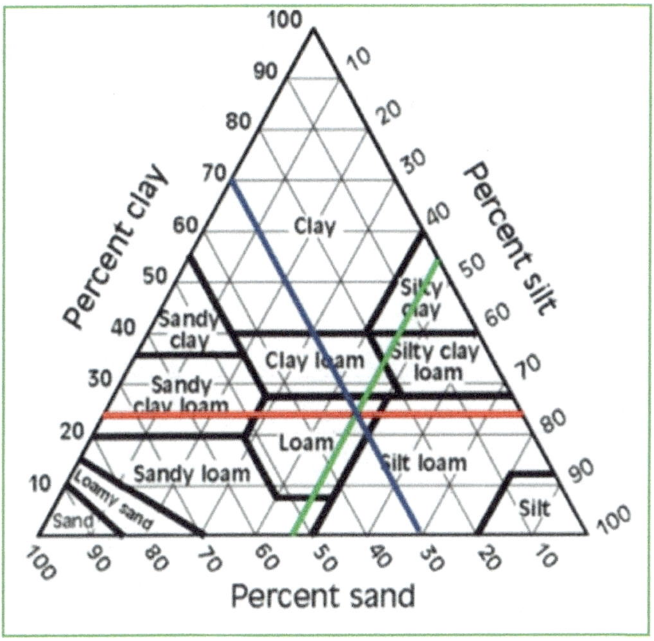

Most soils in Southern USA States will require some form of organic amendments. Adding organic matter to clay and sandy soil can help with:

- Nutrient holding capacity
- Improved drainage
- Reducing compaction

Soil Texture Analysis "The Jar Test" Measurements

Height of sand layer ________inches / cm

Height of silt layer ________inches / cm

Height of clay layer ________inches / cm

TOTAL HEIGHT OF LAYERS ________inches / cm

% SAND=(sand height)/(total height) x 100 =____________ % SAND

% SILT=(silt height)/(total height) x 100 =____________ % SILT

% CLAY=(clay height)/(total height) x 100 =____________ % SILT

Notes:

Soil Testing Process

After testing the soil to make sure it is adequate enough to begin growing, it is important to remain familiar with testing soil to know when newer soil can be added to your space. Simply purchasing "new" soil and mixing with your soil from the season before may not be helpful and can possibly lead to contamination. You will always want to add soil as needed after testing. Use the following chart below when testing your soil during each season.

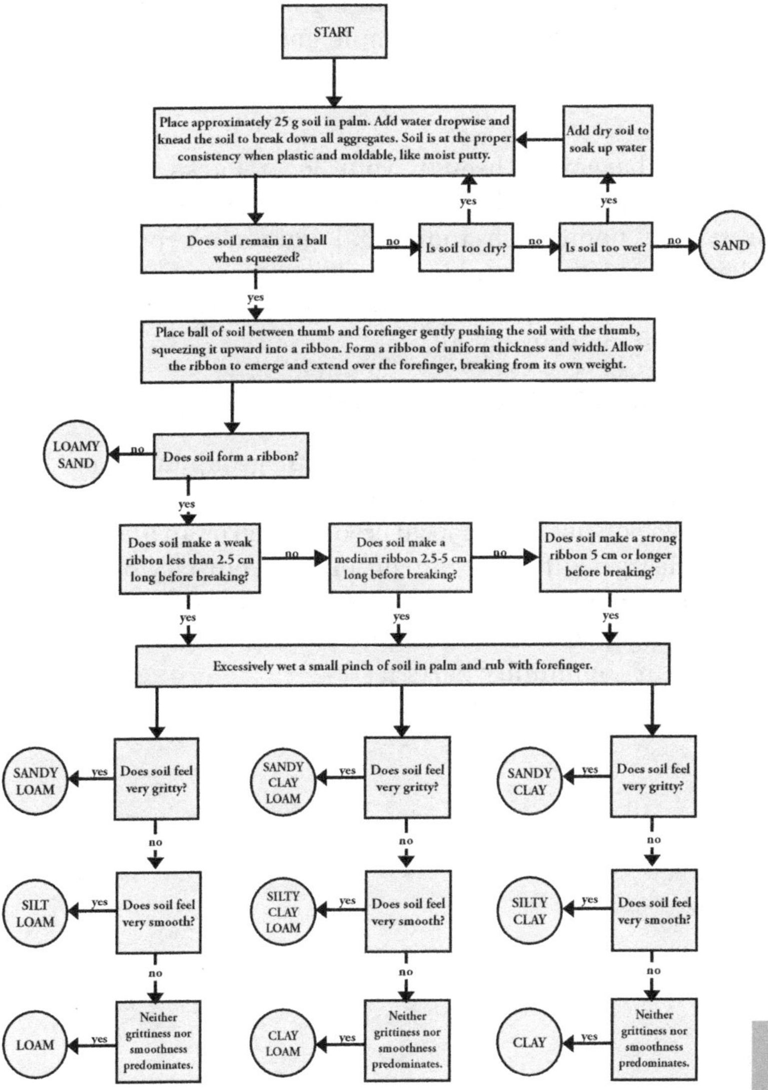

Signing A Lease

Landowners of potential garden sites might be concerned about their liability should someone be injured while working the garden. Your group should be prepared to offer the landowner a lease with a "hold harmless" waiver. This "hold harmless" waiver can simply state that should one of the gardeners be injured as a result of negligence on the part of another gardener, the landowner is "held harmless" and will not be sued. Each gardener should be made aware of this waiver and should be signed in order to obtain a plot in the community garden. A sample gardener agreement form is outlined later in this chapter and can be used as a model for your group.

If you will be going through your local Parks and Recreation Department for establishing your garden, you are accepting liability but upon each individual gardener's personal safety. Gardeners can (and should) sign an agreement taking personal responsibility for safety of themselves and the garden space to avoid liability on your behalf.

8 Obtaining Liability Insurance

Landowners may also require that your group purchase liability insurance. Community gardeners in your area can obtain inexpensive policies from a local credit union or an already existing sustainable agriculture organization via your city or town Parks Department. Once you have a lease and/or agreement signed by the landowner, you're free to put your plans to use and begin starting your community garden.

2 Planning Your Garden

Community members should be involved in the planning, design, and set-up of the garden. Before the design process begins, you should measure your site and make a simple, to-scale site map. Hold two or three garden design meetings at times when interested participants can attend. Make sure that group decisions are recorded in official minutes, or that someone takes accurate notes. This ensures that decisions made can be communicated to others, and progress will not be slowed. A great way to generate ideas and visualize the design is to use simple drawings or photos cut from garden magazines representing the different garden components--flower beds, compost bins, pathways, arbors, etc.--that can be moved around on the map as the group discusses layout.

1. Basic Elements Of A Community Garden

Although there are exceptions to every rule, community gardens should almost always include the following:

At least 10 plots assigned to community members. These should be placed in the sunniest part of the garden. Without plots for individual participation, it is very difficult to achieve long-term community involvement. Raised bed plots, which are more expensive, should be no more than 4 feet wide (to facilitate access to plants from the sides without stepping into the bed), and between 8 and 12 feet long (it is advisable to construct your raised beds in sizes that are found in readily available lumber, or that can be cut without too much waste). In-ground plots can be from 8ft x 4ft up to 5ft x 10 ft. Pathways between beds and plots should be least 3 to 4 feet wide to allow space for wheelbarrows. The soil in both raised bed and in-ground plots should be amended with aged compost or manure to improve its fertility and increase its organic matter content.

A Simple Irrigation System with one hose bib or faucet for every four plots. ***Hand watering with a hose or water jug/can is the most practical and affordable for individual plots*** (and it's almost a necessity when you start plants from seed). Drip and soaker-hose irrigation can be used in all areas of the garden for transplanted and established plants, but especially for deep-rooted fruit trees and ornamentals. If no one in your group is knowledgeable about irrigation, you might need some assistance in designing your irrigation system. Seek out a landscape contractor or nursery or garden center professional to help you develop a basic layout and materials list.

- A fence around the perimeter with a drive-through gate, or open space for a truck to park (in my experience, this is a key element of success). Don't count on eliminating all acts of vandalism or theft, but fencing will help to keep these to tolerably low levels. Having space for a truck to park is important for transporting materials and also loading up things such as dirt each season.

- A tool shed or other structure for storing tools, supplies, and materials (members can also be encouraged to bring their own tools to use independently). Recycled metal shipping containers make excellent storage sheds, and are almost vandal-proof. Contact the Port Authority for leads on where to find them.

- A bench or picnic table where gardeners can sit, relax, and take a break--preferably in shade. If there are no shade trees on the site, a simple arbor can be constructed from wood or pipe, and planted with chayote squash, bougainvillea, grapes, kiwis, or some other vine.

- A sign with the garden's name, sponsors, and a contact person's phone number for more information. If your community is bilingual, include information in those languages.

- A shared composting area for the community gardeners. Wood pallets are easy to come-by and (when stood on-end, attached in a U-shape, and the inside covered with galvanized rabbit-wire) make excellent compost bins.

2. Creating a Garden Budget

Use your design to develop a materials list and cost-out the project. You will need to call-around to get prices on fencing and other items. You might be surprised at the cost. A community garden with just the Basic Elements (listed above) typically costs between $2,500 to $5,000 but can be a low as $200 a year (the majority of costs can and should be covered by plots being rented yearly). At this point, your group might decide to scale back your initial plans and save some design ideas for a "Phase Two" of the garden to make room to add plots and space as funding and interest is more secured.

3. Where to Get Materials and Money

While some start-up funds will be needed through determination and hard work, you can obtain donations of materials for your project. Community businesses might assist, and provide anything from fencing to lumber to plants. The important thing is to ask. Develop a letter that tells merchants about your project and why it's important to the community. Attach your "wish list", but be reasonable. Try to personalize this letter for each business you approach. Drop it off personally with the store manager, preferably with a couple of cute kids who will be gardening! Then, follow-up by phone.

Be patient, persistent, and polite. Your efforts will pay-off with at least some of the businesses you approach. Be sure to thank these key supporters and recognize them on your garden sign, at a garden grand opening, or other special event. Money, which will be needed to purchase items not donated, can be obtained through community fund-raisers such as car washes, craft and rummage sales, sponsored breakfasts, and bake sales. A more direct approach can be requesting donations during local elections in the form of sponsorships.

Finances can also be obtained by writing grants, but be aware grant writing efforts can take six months or longer to yield results, and you must have a fiscal sponsor or agent with tax-exempt 501(c)3 status (such as a church or non-profit corporation) that agrees to administer the funds.

After your garden has opened you can do any of the following to continue adding revenue to your garden to cover expenses:

Renting Out Plots

Renting out plots are a way to cover some costs to operate your garden and help make sure each plot will be taken care of since it's likely a person paying for their plot will take care of it and make best use of their investment.

Adopt-a-Plot

Many people in the area may not be able to pay for their own plot(s). However, there are many who may not want to use a garden plot for themselves but would like to contribute. Allowing members of the community to adopt a plot, will help maintain retention for your garden space and also put on display how the community as a whole is working together.

Selling Seeds and Seedlings

Each season, seeds will be needed to begin growing each plant. Many people in your community may already have a home garden and would be willing to purchase seeds to take home with them. You can purchase a variety of seeds from many sources and may also receive free seeds from donations as you further tap into your community's resources.

While you have a variety of seeds, it can be useful for you to begin planting some seeds and making them available for purchase as each plant grows. Host an event for anyone in the community to purchase seedings to later transplant. Use small events and get-togethers to help sell these plants to raise money, but also fill any remaining spots you may have available in your garden.

Tours

Provide depth to your garden by having access to your garden. Teach and help others learn about the development of the garden, your plans, and use your time to locate each plant and educate on the many benefits each item contains. Providing regular tours can lead to an additional income by either, charging for tours, or create more in-depth conversations about the potential and future of the garden and lead to innumerable opportunities and lifelong connections.

Community-Supported Agriculture (CSA)

Community Supported Agriculture (CSA) is a production and marketing model whereby consumers buy shares of a farm's harvest in advance. You will need a larger space that would operate as a Farm to provide CSA services. Consumers become CSA members by paying an agreed amount at the beginning of the growing season, either in one lump sum or in installments. The annual costs, depend on the length of the harvest season and the variety and quantity of products provided. This upfront payment helps buy the seeds and other inputs needed for the season and provides the farmer an immediate income to begin the season. By paying at the beginning of the season, CSA members share in the risk of production and relieve the farmer of much of the time needed for marketing. This allows the farmer to concentrate on good land stewardship and growing high quality food.

In return for their membership fee, consumers receive a variety of freshly picked produce every week (or bi-weekly). Consumer-members eat healthy, sustainably produced food and have the satisfaction of knowing where it came from and how it was grown. Many CSAs offer on-farm social and educational activities for members, further strengthening their connection to the land and with the farmers who feed them.

Classes

Have a subject matter you want to teach? There are numerous types of classes anyone can teach. Also keep in mind the many teaching opportunities available upon starting your garden where you can invite many volunteers who can also stick around for a class or plan to attend one in the future.

Some examples of classes you can host:

- Basic gardening
- Composting 101
- How to start your seedlings
- Transplanting
- Soil testing
- Arts and crafts
- Go over local resources available within the community
- Health and nutrition
- Disease prevention

4. Make Sure Your Garden Infrastructure Is In Place

If you have not yet formed a garden club, now is the time to do so. It's also time to establish garden rules, develop a garden application form for those who wish to participate, set up a bank account, and determine what garden dues will be if these things have not already been done. This is also the time to begin having monthly meetings if you have not already done so. Also, if you haven't already contacted your city councilperson, he or she can be helpful in many ways including helping your group obtain city services such as trash pick-up. Their staff can also help you with community organizing and soliciting for material donations.

5. Get Growing!

Many new garden groups make the mistake of remaining in the planning, design, and fundraising stage for an extended period of time. There is a fine line between planning well and over planning. After several months of the initial research, designing, planning, and outreach efforts, group members will very likely be feeling frustrated and will begin to wonder if all their efforts will ever result in a garden. That's why it's important to plant something on your site as soon as possible. People need to see visible results, or they will begin to lose interest in the project. To keep the momentum going, initiate the following steps even if you are still seeking donations and funds or your project (but not until you have signed a lease and obtained insurance).

*****Possible Additions to Your Garden Plan*****

- A small fruit tree orchard, whose care and harvest can be shared by all the members. The orchard can also create shade for people as well as shade-loving plants.
- Perimeter landscaping, which can focus on drought tolerant flowers and shrubs, plants which attract butterflies and hummingbirds, or roses and other flowers suitable for cutting bouquets. Herbs are also well-suited to perimeter landscaping and help to create barriers to unwanted pest insects who do not like the smell of their essential oils.
- A children's area, which can include special small plots for children, a sand box, and play equipment.
- A meeting area, which could range from a semi-circle of hay bales or tree stumps, to a simple amphitheater built of recycled, broken concrete. Building a shade structure above would be beneficial as well.
- A community bulletin board where rules, meeting notices, and other important information can be posted
- Artwork! Art can make this space livelier and add a natural element to the garden. Also gives a chance to engage with local artists to collaborate. Artwork will cultivate creativity and give space to enhance the garden by allowing the community to express themselves through creating visualizations to help enhance the space before, during, and after plants have grown.

Maintaining Site

How many workdays you need will depend on the size of the site, and how much and what kind of debris are on site.

Install The Irrigation System

Without water, you can't grow anything. So, get this key element into place as soon as possible. There are plenty of opportunities for community involvement--from digging trenches to laying out PVC pipes. If not an irrigation system, having multiple rain barrels and watering cans available for gardeners to use will be necessary. You can purchase a water barrel, watering pot, and accessories for approximately $75-$100.

Plant Something

Once you have water, there are many options for in-garden action. Stake out beds and pathways by marking them with stakes and twine. Mulch pathways. If your fence isn't in yet, some people might still want to accept the risk of vandalism and get their plots started. You can also plant shade and fruit trees and begin to landscape the site. If you do not yet have a source of donated plants, or don't wish to risk having them vandalized, plant annual flower seeds which will grow quickly and can be replaced later. Continue to construct the garden as materials and funds become available.

Final Step: Celebrate!

At this point, your ideas and hard work have finally become a community garden! Be sure to take time to celebrate. Have a grand opening, or some other fun event to give everyone who helped to make this happen, a special thank-you. This is the time to give all those who gave donated materials or time a special certificate, bouquet, or other form of recognition.

Troubleshooting Potential Problems/Issues

All community gardens will experience problems somewhere along the way. Don't get discourage--get organized. The key to success for community gardens is not only preventing problems from ever occurring, but also working together to solve them when they do inevitably occur. In my experience, these are some of the most common problems that "crop-up" in community gardens, and my suggestions for solving them.

1. Vandalism

Most gardens experience occasional vandalism. The best action you can take is to replant immediately. Generally, the vandals become bored after a while and stop. Good community outreach, especially to youth and the garden's immediately neighbors is also important. Most important--don't get to discouraged. It happens. Get over it and keep going. What about barbed wired or razor wire to make the garden more secure? My advice--don't. It's bad for community relations, looks awful, and is sometimes illegal to install without a permit. If you need more physical deterrents to keep vandals out, plant bougainvillea or pyracantha along your fence, their thorns will do the trick!

2. Security

Invite the community officer from your local precinct or Ward to a garden meeting to get their suggestions on making the garden more secure. Community officers can also be a great help in solving problems with garden vandalism, and dealing with anyone who may purposely make attempts to vandalize the garden directly. Also connecting with neighbors and people in the area that can notify you of any mischief will eventually become your primary source of information.

Note: It is not conducive to putting in a dummy camera or even a "Camera In Use" sign up as there can be legal issues that arise and additional laws to follow. If a dummy camera overlooks private property or is directed towards a window, there could be specific laws you will have to be aware of and follow. So, if you place a sign or install a dummy camera, you will still have to put the time and effort into following laws. At that point, it would make more sense to invest your time and money into a system or local individuals that can take on this responsibility to help improve the safety of your garden.

3. Communication

Communicating clear and well-enforced garden rules and a strong garden president can go a long way towards minimizing misunderstandings in the garden. But communication problems do arise. It's the job of the garden club to resolve those issues. If it's something not clearly spelled out in the rules, the membership can take a vote to add new rules and make modifications to existing rules. Language barriers are a very common source of misunderstandings. Garden club leadership should make every effort to have a translator at garden meetings where participants are bilingual--perhaps a family member of one of the garden members who speaks the language will offer to help.

4. Trash / Waste Management

It's important to get your compost system going right away and get some training for gardeners on how to use it. If gardeners don't compost, large quantities of waste will begin to build up, create an eyesore, and could hurt your relationships with neighbors and the property owner. Waste can also become a fire hazard. Make sure gardeners know how to sort trash properly, what to compost, and what to recycle. Trash cans placed in accessible areas are helpful to keep a neat and tidy garden.

5. Gardener Drop-Out

There has been, and probably always will be, a high rate of turnover in community gardens. Often, people sign up for plots and then don't follow through. Remember, gardening is hard work for some people, especially in the heat of summer. Be sure to have a clause in your gardener agreement which states gardeners forfeit their right to their plot if they don't plant it within one month, or if they don't maintain it. While gardeners should be given every opportunity to follow through, if after several reminders either by letter or phone nothing changes, it is time for the club to reassign the plot. It is also advisable that every year, the leadership conduct a renewed community outreach campaign by contacting churches and other groups in the neighborhood to let them know about the garden and that plots are available.

6. Weeds

Gardeners tend to visit their plots less during the winter, and lower participation, combined with rain, tends to create a huge weed problem in January, February, and March. Remember, part of your agreement with the landowner is that you will maintain the lot and keep weeds from taking over. In the late summer/early fall, provide gardeners with a workshop or printed material about what can be grown in a fall and winter garden. Also, schedule garden workdays for the spring in advance since you know you'll need them at the end of winter to clear weeds. If you anticipate that plots will be untended during the winter, apply a thick layer of mulch or hay to the beds and paths to reduce weed proliferation.

SAMPLE Community Garden Contract

(Information in (bold parentheses) is to be determined by individual garden, provide info, and contact info about garden and contributing organizations).

Introduction:

A. The (organization/garden manager) is the highest governing authority at the (Name) Community Garden.

B. Breaking any rules, terms, and conditions is cause for exclusion from the garden and loss of your plot. 1. You will receive one verbal warning from the garden manager. 2. If no response or correction has been made, you will receive written notice two weeks later. 3. In another two weeks, if no response or correction has been made, you will receive written final notification that you have forfeited your gardening privileges and plot. 4. You will be allowed to reapply for another garden plot only after one year, and only at the discretion of the garden manager.

Rules, Terms, and Condition for Participation If accepted as a gardener, I will abide by the following rules, terms, and conditions:

1. I use this garden at the sole discretion of (Name of) Community Garden. I agree to abide by its policies and practices.

2. The fee for the use of the garden is (Dollar Amount) per plot, per year (January 1 – December 31), due on or before January 1). There are no refunds.

3. Once I have been assigned a plot, I will cultivate and install my plants within three weeks.

4. My plot is (8ft x 4ft – this is standard size. Other sizes are acceptable and at the discretion of the Garden Coordinator). I will not expand my plot beyond this measurement or into paths or other plots unless approved by Garden Coordinator. I will keep all my plants within the limits of my garden plot and will not allow any plants to grow more than six feet high. I must keep my plot free of weeds, pests, and diseases.

5. I will keep my plot, paths, and surrounding areas clean and neat. I will not bring household trash and leave it at the Community Garden.

6. If I now have more than one plot, I will remain responsible for each assigned plot.

7. I will not plant any illegal plant. I will not come to the garden while under the influence of alcohol or illegal drugs.

8. I am solely responsible for the behavior of my guests. They must follow all rules, terms, and conditions stated here.

9. I will water my plot according to water-wise guidelines.

10. I will attend the regular (bi-monthly) garden club meetings. If workshops are offered, I will attend at least one of each of the following topics: soil preparation and maintenance, watering the vegetable garden, and pest and disease control.

11. I will not apply any pesticides in the garden without the approval of the garden manager.

12. I will not make duplicate keys of any locks at the garden or give my key or lock combination to another person.

13. I will not take food or plants from other gardeners' plots. I will not take anything from the garden that is not rightfully mine.

14. I will respect other gardeners, and I will not use abusive or profane language or discriminate against others.

15. I will work to keep the garden a happy, secure, and enjoyable place where all participants can garden and socialize peacefully in a neighborly manner.

16. I forfeit my right to sue the owner of the property Commitment.

I have read and understand the application and accept these rules, terms, and conditions stated above for the participation in the (Name) Community Garden

Signed ______________________________ Date:____________

Gardener Approved: __________________ Date:____________

3 Gardening Planning & Spacing

Start by thinking about what you want to grow and make a list of all the fruits, vegetables, and herbs you want to grow; flowers can be included as well. If your list is long, start by narrowing down your list to what you can grow in smaller spaces and use local farmer's markets to get additional foods (and seeds) during the growing season. Use the Square Foot Gardening Guide below to determine how many squares each type of plant requires and how tall each may grow. Make a sketch of you garden bed and get started.

Unless you're a very experienced gardener or have a lot of land to use, there are two primary methods for gardening your growing space:

1. **Square Foot Gardening**
2. **Transplanting**

Note: square foot gardening is how most gardens are formatted however, taking the time to measure out so that each plot is even within the garden plot is what is referred to as "Square Foot Gardening". Also, Transplanting can be done within Square Foot Gardening or anywhere else that provides enough space for the plant to begin growing close to its full potential.

Square Foot Gardening

I would highly recommend using the square foot method to plan your garden; not only in its beginning stages, but each season you will want to get the most out of the space you have. In the late 1970's (American Gardener, Engineer, Inventor, and Author) Mel Bartholomew developed the square foot gardening method. This method was proven to produce a greater harvest in less space (and less work!). In Square Foot Gardening, the plants are arranged by blocks instead of rows. Each block contains a different vegetable, herb, or flower. By using this technique, you can easily clear and replant squares throughout the season without disturbing other areas of the garden.

You will notice in the image in the next pages that I have marked off the sides of the raised bed into one-foot increments (plot size is 8ft x 4ft). When you are ready to plant, take a stick or handle of a garden tool and lay it across the bed to mark to the one directly opposite on the other side of the bed. Push it lightly into the soil until lit leaves an indentation in the soil. Continue marking the soil around the bed until you have formed a grid pattern on the soil. Now you are ready to plant.

The number of seeds or plants that are placed in each square depends on how large the plant grows and how much space it needs to develop properly. Small plants, such as carrots, do not require much room so you can plant about 14-16 carrots in a square. Collards require one square for each plant; and a large tomato plant needs 2-3 squares. Once your garden is planted, you can easily follow the progress of a single square, see when weeds invade and remove them, determine when to water individual plants and see any potential plant pest problems. I hope that by offering this method, it will help you grow a large amount of produce, and help to save time on garden maintenance.

Be sure to water the seeds gently right after you plant them. This is best completed by using a spray bottle or mist nozzle on a hose. Some seeds are very small and close to the top of the soil, that excess water from a cup or hose can wash the seeds away. It is important to keep the soil moist, but not soaking them as seeds germinate. The compost that is used in raised beds can dry out fairly quickly. For this reason, it is important to water the seeds gently each morning until they germinate. Try to avoid watering in the middle of the day when soil moisture evaporates quickly due to sunlight exposure.

After seeds germinate, you may have more than one plant in a single spot. Decide which plant seems to be the strongest and "thin out" the others. Thin your seeds by gently pulling out shoots you do not want or carefully clip them off with small scissors at the base of the shoot.

Example of Square Foot Gardening

Use thumb tacks and yarn to make a "grid" for your plants. Measure out ach sections first to make sure each side is even. This plot is 8ft x 4ft. you can measure out before where you want to put each tack, or feel free to just measure by eye as not every plant will grow exactly within the confines of each square. You will want to be as even as possible so that you do not waste any space or end up compromising a plant from growing in a smaller space.

Transplanting:

You've probably seen smaller plants inside of these small black squares before, right? Sitting on a counter somewhere or by the gardening section at a retail business. May have wondered what each plant is and if you wanted to purchase any. These plants are what we refer to as "seedlings" that have begun to sprout and are close to the point where they can become transplanted into a larger pot, garden bed, or into the ground.

To transplant, you will simply have to dig a hole in the soil, slightly larger than the container in which the seedlings are growing. Carefully take out the entire plant and surrounding soil from the container or pot. If you happen to see a clump of tangled roots at the bottom of the root bail, gently pick these loose and separate them from being tangled with one another. Next step is to place the plant carefully in the hole you dug. With vegetable transplants you can bury the plant up to the first set of leaves that are growing; this will also help prevent the plant from drying out too quickly. Pat down the soil firmly around the plant so that the roots are in contact with the soil. Then you will want to smooth the soil around the stem so that the surface of the soil drains slightly towards the plant. This will help the plant collect moisture throughout the day.

Water the base (not the leaves) of each seedling immediately after transplanting to help the plant adjust and connect with its new environment. Make sure to water regularly, especially if transplanting mid-summer. Newly transplanted seedlings often suffer from shock and look "sad" for a few days but will perk up after they adjust to their new environment and connect with the soil in your garden bed. To lessen the chances of shock happening to your plants, transplant your plants on a cloudy day and/or early in the morning.

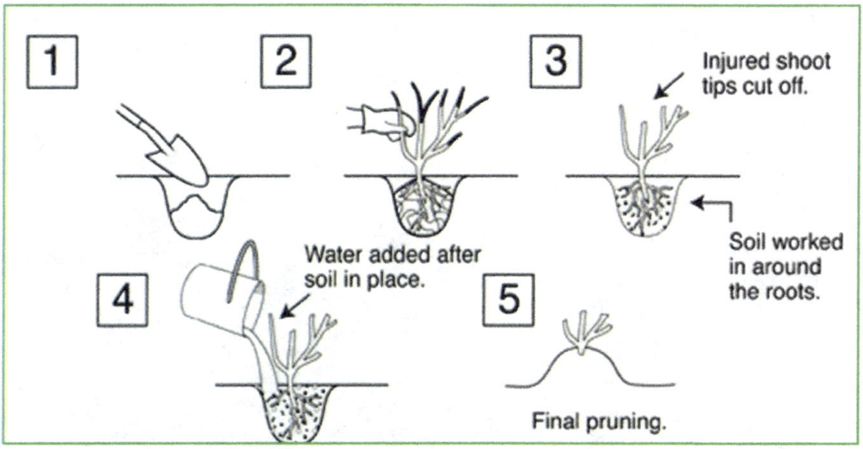

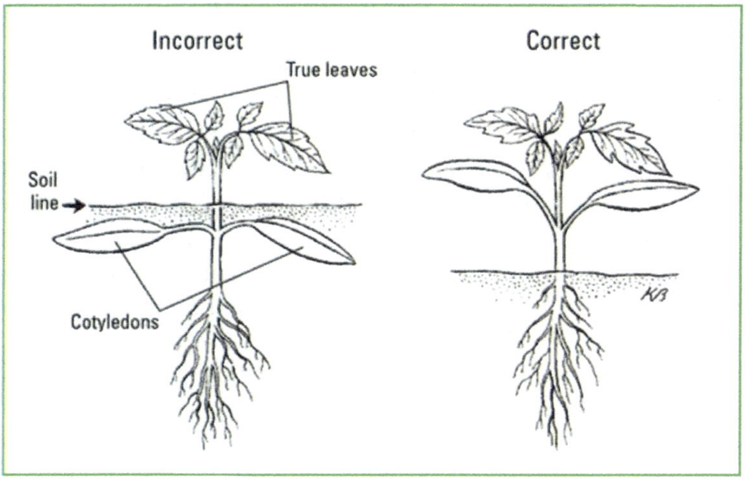

Following the instructions above should help you plan for a terrific growing season! Transplanting correctly can be the difference between having an abundance of fresh produce growing within your garden, and an underachieving gardening season where many plants only begin to sprout and never grow to their full potential.

Labeling:

Label what you have planted in each square so you will remember the location of each plant. Simple labels such as the ones on the next page are helpful as they are easy to write on and can also withstand various weather conditions. Including the planting date on the label will let you know how long ago you planted and when you should expect to see the first sprouts. Knowing where each of your plants are located also help you provide each plant with an adequate amount of water each needs as certain plants require more water than others, and also help you observe what each plant looks like as it grows which will help you in the future with identifying plants and with determining the health of your plants.

Spacing Your Plants:

Determining plant spacing is crucial to your plants' health. Adequate spacing is not only needed for their roots to grow, but plants need enough space to also absorb sunlight daily. There are several methods to follow such as Square Foot gardening, Planting in rows, and Intensive Gardening. Most plants will come with labels and/or instructions that provide spacing, sunlight, germination (when a plant will begin to grow), and the estimated height each plant will reach; height is important to know to plan for not blocking sunlight from other plants and determining if any tools such as garden stakes, trellis, or pole, are needed to help your plant continue to grow to its' potential.

When using the Square Foot Gardening method, plants are spread differently than they are in traditional row methods. View the images below to help see how to space your plants.

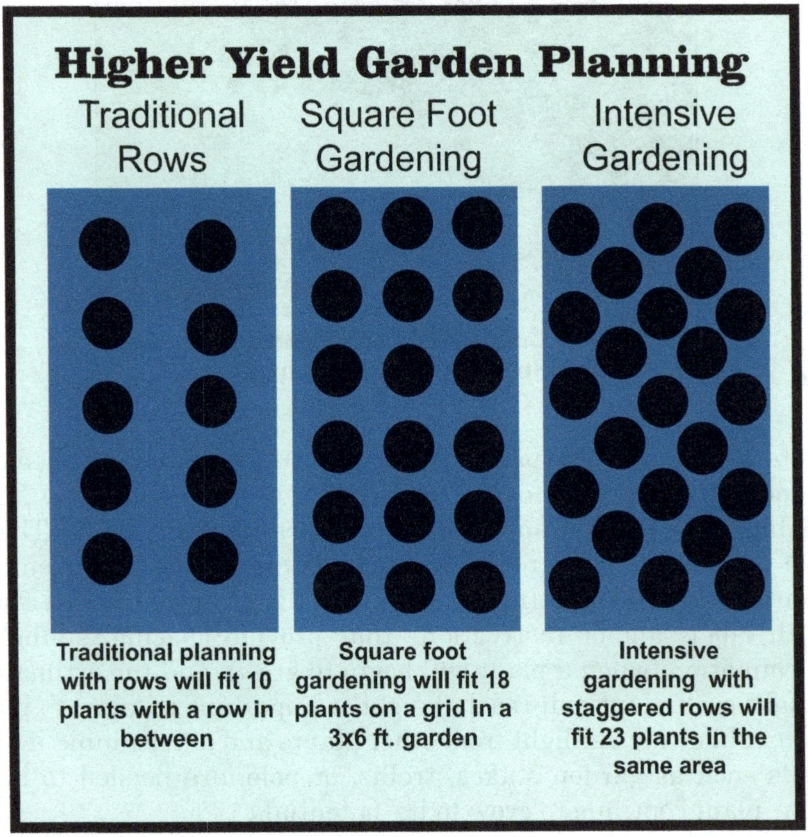

Traditional Row gardens use rows with unused garden space between each row of plants for walking. When there's not enough space to walk in between, other gardening methods such as Square Foot and Intensive Gardening can be considered. Unless you have a large garden area, the rows in between the plants waste a lot of gardening area. An average 3x6 foot garden planted with the traditional row arrangement will fit only ten plants with about 12 inch spacing between plants.

Another method commonly used in raised beds and backyard vegetable gardens is the **Square Foot Gardening** method. In this method, the gardener lays out a grid in the garden with each square in the grid measuring one square foot. Therefore, in a 3x6 foot garden, you would be able to fit 18 plants. On one hand, this allows roots to spread and gives your enough space for your plants to grow. On the other hand, you may have some additional space that's not being utilized.

Intensive Gardening still follows the suggested plant spacing of 12 inches, but staggers the rows of plants to make use of the lost corner space in square foot gardening. The spacing for plants in this arrangement are measured at an angle, allowing even more plants to fit in the area. This 3x6 garden will hold 23 plants that require 12 inch spacing!

Keep in mind what types of plants you plan to use to determine your plant spacing. Some plants that are taller require more spacing due to their roots being deeper, and due to the fact, you do not want a plant towering over another plant and creating additional shade which will lead to your plant not getting enough sunlight.

More plants mean more produce, and more produce means more yield from the space that you have. Just always remain mindful of what you are planting and not adding too many plants so that their roots do not interfere with one another, and you end up having your plants not maturing.

These are just a few of the many ways to increase your yields, and use as an outline for the space you and your gardeners will be using each season.

Ideal Timeline for Starting A Community Garden

Summer-Fall

1. Get your group together.
2. Define your goals.
3. Start to develop your garden management plan.
4. Assess options and pick a site. Make arrangements with landowner if needed.

Fall

1. Continue outreach, generating interest.
2. Start designing your garden site.
3. Start drafting a list of supplies, materials and other resources needed and begin to build a budget.

Fall-Winter

1. Finalize overall garden design (budget-dependent details).
2. Finalize budget.
3. Start fundraising and looking for donations ($ and in-kind).
4. Continue garden management plan. Determine governance, rules, roles, and responsibilities.

Winter

1. Continue fundraising.
2. Obtain insurance if needed.
3. Continue outreach. Look for volunteers (to help develop site) and gardeners.
4. Continue garden design and layout.

Winter-Spring

1. Finalize garden management plan and prepare for your gardeners by creating forms and guides.
2. Organize the gardeners: orientation, applications, waivers, fees, scheduling, etc.
3. Finalize garden design and layout.
4. Gather all remaining materials needed—plants, seeds, tools, compost, etc.

Spring

1. Prepare and develop site.

4 Warren Park Community Garden (Lynn, MA)

The Warren Park Community Garden in Lynn, MA was a garden I created in the spring of 2016 when I simply wanted to grow my own foods close to my home. My home at the time (and for close to the previous 21 years) is just one city block away from where the garden is located. I did some in person learning on how to transplant, grow, and space out the items I planned on growing from a local garden that was already established. I figured I could work with my own plot and help a few other people do the same.

I originally wanted to create this garden space back when I was in college but was rejected due to this section of Lynn, MA being labeled as a "high risk and dangerous" area by local city officials. However, I persisted and connected with like-minded individuals and organizations (The Food Project, and the Lynn Food & Fitness Alliance; later on, setting the development of "Lynn Grows" where everyone works collaboratively). We came together to set forth a more formal proposal and identifying logistics including, having access to compost and dirt, who will be responsible for building each plot, and identifying a Garden Coordinator(which happened to be myself) who would take on recruitment of gardeners, setting ground rules, and coordinating events as well as delegating responsibilities to the other gardeners.

Here Was Our Initial Letter Proposal

Proposed Community Garden at Warren Park

(Located on the southwest side of Lynn Commons, one block from Commercial St.)

The neighborhood surrounding Warren Park is comprised mainly of multi-family housing with limited access to yard space. Surveys conducted in summer 2017 indicate neighboring residents are supportive of a community garden and receptive to the conversion of unused park space for this purpose.

An unusable tennis court at Warren Park can accommodate dozens of raised garden beds. We propose installing approximately twelve beds in the sunniest area of the court. Neighbors have committed to gardening in 4 of the beds. Lynn Food and Fitness Alliance (LFFA) is confident that with additional community outreach all beds can be filled for the 2018 gardening season.

The Food Project will fund and install the garden beds, including the cost of compost to fill the beds. LFFA is working with neighbors to determine an appropriate water source. Garden beds will not be built until a source of water is identified.

The yellow outline below indicates the proposed garden space.

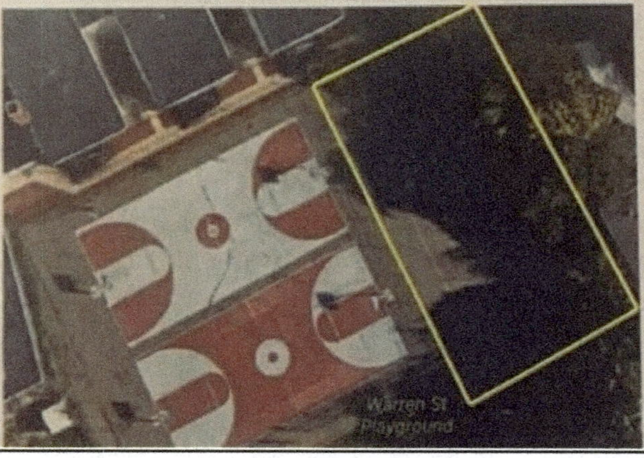

In this proposal listed how neighbors would garden in 4 of the beds, while I occupy one of the plots and another plot is dedicated to the Day Care next door for a total of 6 out of 10 plots being occupied prior to opening. This displayed that the garden would have each plot occupied while leaving space for a few people to join once the garden was ready. Partnering with a local nonprofits and organizations, The Food Project and the Lynn Food and Fitness Alliance made it easier to delegate tasks and create a network to connect services (water source, compost, and promotion) within the city and remain open to applying for specific grants that could cover additional costs.

My plans to create this Community Garden was originally denied a total of 17 times before the 18th time it was approved to begin connecting resources for its' creation. Rejection of this plan was due to the location being in a "violent area in close proximity of having the highest number of murders and violent crimes within the city". I used this to propose that if this Garden does not "work" then we come together to identify what may work while also tracking a decrease in violent crimes in the area. I also proposed how more foot traffic into the park and regular cleaning would deter crime and reduce the amount of littering in the area. Also, included how the Day Care next door had its gate closed due to activity in the park during the day (drug sales, drug use, alcohol drinking, and littering) would be able to expand the space they had access to for their kids which would result in improved behaviors and retention.

Members within the neighborhood began growing many plants and started several small home gardens in the area to help promote the need and interest (at least for this location). Using the community's efforts, we were eventually able to come together in a central location (The Warren Park Community Garden) and begin to share ideas, recipes, growing tips, and share/trade items we all grew in our plots. Crime decreased considerable in the area overall and we were able to continue growing the garden, host basketball tournaments, and use the playground without many challenges.

Here I am measuring out the plots before our initial construction of the garden (look at that beard!)

Year 1

Through an application process, we started out with ten 8ft x 4ft garden beds. We scanned the entire community and chose to start with ten plots so we can maximize the starting potential of this space while also accurately assessing the need and interest of the community and their desire to grow their own produce. Those on the waitlist were referred to nearby gardens but more importantly, they were able to remain connected via community gardening events and activities, and being provided regular updated information about local Farmer's Markets, plant sales, and being invited to local steering committee meetings where we discussed future plans, current needs, and sharing ideas.

Year 2 (Adding Additional Garden Beds)

From Year 1 to Year 2 we expanded from having the same gardeners and practiced our community outreach efforts by connecting with those on the waitlist and giving preference to those who attended regular committee meetings. We also worked to address the needs of availability and those who presented a greater need of food insecurity and financial constraints. I planned events around local elections to do the additional beds as I knew we would have extra help, interest, and could accept donations and free promotion via social media and local news outlets. We were able to build and fill all of the new plots in just a few hours with the additional help of the community. With us not having to do the work ourselves, we were able to branch out and speak to those who volunteered their time about our efforts and vision. We also used this time to provide insight on future plans we had and free information packets about the work we have all done individually and collectively together.

Soon after expanding the garden with the new plots, we noticed how many Realters in the area were including "access to local community garden" in their listings. This does not present a barrier, however, it meant additional profits for individual Realtors. We invested our own money, time, and efforts to improve this area, so if anyone should benefit from this space, it would be the community.

After meeting and evaluating our stance, we were able to decide how we can turn this into a benefit for the community. With market rates for housing going up in the area, the estimated value of the neighborhood also increased, partly thanks to establishing and growing the Warren Park Community Garden. What was determined by our research was that, if the overall value of the area increased (while crimes were also decreasing), then more taxes would be getting paid over time, which would make the area (and the city as a whole) become eligible for a deeper pool grants to be applied for. The City provided us insight on grants they were showing interest in applying for and we were able to express our thoughts and ideas. We mutually agreed upon a grant that was a City-Wide grant for restoring parks and playgrounds, where Warren Park would receive the majority of the grant money available.

With this money we were able to do additional clean-ups of the garden, improve our water-irrigation system, install a brand-new playground structure, provide additional repairs and upgrades to the Day Care next door, and completely renovate the basketball courts with new paint, lines, and backboards.

Final Result!

Overall plan for expansion in phases with flexible timelines for each phase

We ended up drifting a bit away from our original plans but kept use of space so additional garden beds could still be added over time. Raised beds for elderly residents and/or those who may use a walker or wheelchair.

5 Composting 101

Before we begin planning for larger areas for your growing space, something to properly understand (and master) is, Composting.

What Is Compost?

Compost is organic matter – like fruit and vegetable scraps and other kitchen scraps – that has decomposed through the actions of various microbes (bacteria, fungi, etc.) and other organisms (like earthworms). Scraps, along with brown materials like leaves, sawdust, are added to a pile or bin, turned regularly to incorporate air, and distribute material, and left to decompose over time. The material heats up through microbial action ("cooks") and eventually turns into usable compost – a rich, fertile, soil-like material that can be used for home gardening and farming. Depending on the size of the compost system, compost creation can take weeks to up to a year.

How to Set Up Your Compost Bin or Pile

Compost bins or piles can be set up in many ways – from big municipal systems to small home bins. Choose the type and size that works best for you and your garden size.

The Carbon/Nitrogen Ratio

Scraps to compost fall into two basic categories: carbon-rich "browns" and nitrogen-rich "greens." You need more carbon in your mix than you need nitrogen, with an optimum carbon/nitrogen ratio of about 30:1. If there is too much carbon (browns), decomposition will slow down. If there is too much nitrogen (greens), your pile may end up unsatisfactory.

Generally, meeting this ratio means adding about one part Brown for every two parts Green, giving the decomposers a balanced diet with enough energy and nutrients to eat through everything you compost.

Carbon-rich "browns" tend to be dry, woody materials. Nitrogen-rich "greens" are usually colorful (think fruits and veggies) and usually a little moist. Here are few examples:

BROWNS (CARBON-RICH)

- Dried leaves
- Sawdust and woodchips (make sure these are from untreated wood)
- Shredded black and white newspaper
- Egg cartons
- Cardboard
- Dead, dried-out plants (disease-free)
- Tree bark
- Straw
- Peanut shells

GREENS (NITROGEN-RICH)

- Fruit and vegetable kitchen scraps
- Coffee grounds and tea bags
- Green garden cuttings
- Fresh leaves and flowers
- Grass clippings

The carbon/nitrogen ratio balancing act can be as simple or complicated as you like. The easiest approach is to stick to the basic 2:1 (two parts green to one part brown) recipe. But if you're striving for optimal compost efficiency, or want to achieve a specific soil quality for your gardening needs, check out The Compost Info Guide (https://www.compost-info-guide.com/greens.htm) to find the exact C/N ratios for a wide variety of compostables.

Adding Material to Your Compost

For maximum efficiency, shred, or chop food scraps before adding them to your compost whenever possible – the smaller the pieces, the faster and more effectively your compostables will decompose. When you add yard trimmings, for instance, use clippers to cut stems into shorter lengths. Always rip apart newspapers, cardboard, and paper egg cartons before composting to distribute the carbon content more evenly.

Because you need to add browns (carbon) to your compost every time you add food scraps and other greens, it may be handy to keep a container of dry, carbon-rich materials near your compost pile/bin.

Turning Your Compost

Periodically turn your compost with a pitchfork or shovel so the new material ends up on the warm interior of your compost pile.

Turning your compost also infuses your pile with oxygen (also known as "Aeration"), which is essential for the aerobic bacteria that help decompose material. If you have not added materials to your compost heap in a while, make sure you still turn the compost every so often. If the material gets too dry, you can water it with a hose (moisture content should be about 50 percent) to maintain the moisture that the composting microbes need.

<u>*Other Tips for Healthy Compost***</u>**

Compost Not Warming Up Enough?

Compost needs to get hot so that material breaks down sufficiently – depending on the size of your pile, temperatures can be as hot as 115F to 180F. If your compost pile is well maintained but not warming up, here are some tips:

- Try adding more browns. Carbon is an energy source that bacteria will devour, heating up their environment.

- You can also try covering your compost to retain more heat. Add a layer of dirt, straw, or other browns to trap heat. (Covering has the added benefit of deterring bugs around your pile.)
- Using a compost bin or barrel will usually heat itself when out in direct sunlight. You just want to plan for what size and/or how many depending on the garden size and land space you are using.

Compost Odor

Smells are a bad sign for your compost. Please avoid adding meat and oily foods to your pile, which can attract pests, and can make your compost unsuitable for using in the future. Your compost should not give off odors. Strong, foul smells usually indicate that the aerobic bacteria in your compost are struggling for one reason or another. Remedy your compost's stench with these quick pointers:

- Turn your compost: You may have a heap full of stinky anaerobic bacteria if you are not turning your compost frequently. Try turning your compost every few days to infuse the pile with oxygen so that odor-free aerobic bacteria thrive, and anaerobic bacteria do not.
- Add more browns: If your pile smells like ammonia, you've added too much green. Try adding more browns for each part green to for a balanced carbon/nitrogen ratio.
- Top with dirt: You can prevent smells by adding an extra layer of dirt or other brown covering over the top after turning and mixing in more browns.

What to Compost and How to Do It

Dumping food waste and other organic matter into landfills just doesn't make sense. Trapped under layers of garbage, these materials not only release massive amounts of pollutants such as methane,they also become unavailable where they're needed most – back within the soil.

Composting instead of trashing food waste and other organics slashes environmental impacts and transforms otherwise squandered scraps into a useful resource. Dark, moist, nutrient-rich compost is a perfect fertilizer, free of pollutants, chemicals – and cost! For green thumbs and local farmers, compost adds invaluable organic structure and nutrients to the soil, and for everyone else, healthy soil = healthier foods = healthier planet.

Whether you keep your own compost pile, are lucky enough to have municipal curbside composting, or drop off your scraps at a composting facility, you'll need to know what to compost – and what to avoid adding to the compost pile.

What Exactly Can You Compost?

Food scraps, yard trimmings and paper products are the most common ingredients used to feed compost heaps – but plenty of other organic waste can be added, too.

As a rule, any item that was once alive or was derived from living matter can be composted. However, there are reasons to limit what you compost, particularly because the types of materials you use can optimize decomposition, deter pests, and keep things from getting stinky. Avoiding toxic, diseased, chemical-contaminated wastes is also important.

Good Scraps for Composting

Whether you're composting in your backyard, or sending scraps to a municipal compost operation, some items are nearly always acceptable for compost. Here's a list of common items you can toss in your compost pile without a second thought:

FOOD SCRAPS

- Fruit and vegetable peels and scrap
- Plant Leftovers from Meals
- Tea bags (remove the staple!)
- Coffee grounds and filters

- Grains (breads, cereals, rice, pastas, etc.)
- Nut Shells
- Fruit pits
- Bottle corks

YARD TRIMMINGS

- Leaves, straw, pine needles
- Fresh or dried grass (as with all items on this list – chemical-free only)
- Flower and plant clippings
- Weeds that have not gone to seed
- Houseplants and potting soil
- Wood ash

PAPER PRODUCTS

- Paper items (napkins, paper towels, shredded brown bags, etc.)
- Shredded cardboard boxes
- Shredded black and white newspaper
- Non-glossy junk mail
- Bedding from hamster/gerbil/rabbit cages
- Paper coffee filters

Bad Scraps for Composting

Don't put inorganic materials in your compost! While this may seem obvious, sometimes scraps can be contaminated with synthetics that can mess up the composting process, so take extra care. Any garden bits that may have come in contact with pesticides, weed killers or other inorganic products should be avoided, for instance. Additional common items to avoid include plastics, medicines, colored paper, and cleaning chemicals.

For more guidance on what you can compost, view this list of 100 compostables (https://www.smallfootprintfamily.com/100-things-you-can-compost) and visit the Can I Compost This? Website (https://www.compostthis.co.uk/).

Where to Keep Your Scraps

When you compost, separating your organics from other waste materials means reducing odors and other issues (like unwanted vermin). But you still need a place to keep those scraps before they hit the compost pile or get dumped into a municipal composting bin.

1. *The Freezer or Fridge:* Freezing and refrigerating compostables has one major perk: No matter how late you are "taking out the compost," frozen scraps will never decompose and refrigerated scraps will be virtually odorless, so you'll never need to worry about smells or attracting unwanted guests.

2. *Under the Sink or On the Counter:* If you don't have room in your freezer, or will be discarding waste every few days, storing kitchen scraps under your sink or on your counter may be a convenient option. To keep scraps fresher between the time you save them and the time you actually dump them on a compost pile, you'll need a container that's easy to keep clean, seal and store out of the way.

Clean and Simple Collecting

Chop up bulky scraps to get the most volume out of your bag or bin. Another option to reduce your volume is to avoid composting leftovers or preparation waste altogether. You can find plenty of recipes for reusing leftovers and commonly discarded, yet perfectly edible scraps like kale stems online.

If you keep your scraps at room temperature, fruit flies are bound to make an appearance every so often. Peelings, especially from fruit, often attract fruit flies, so refrigerating ripe produce and freezing the peels as soon as possible can help deter flies. To keep flies at bay in your countertop bucket, try lining your bin with newspaper or soiled paper towels to reduce moisture. You can also sprinkle small amounts of baking soda to curtail odors, add melon pieces or rub vinegar on the top of your counter. of your container. The best way to avoid flies and smells, however, is to freeze your food scraps – or simply take your compost out regularly and wash the reusable container every time.

6 Lynn Tech Farm

With a growing interest within the community for growing their own foods (and a very long waitlist at each community garden), we all began looking for additional locations for a community garden or larger space to accommodate the needs of the community and continue our efforts to expand. As we were searching throughout the city, we received word that where there was already a growing space occupied by The Food Project, there were bids being placed to purchase by real estate developers. There were also plans of a potential Charter School placing a bid on the land as they were looking to expand. With this news, we immediately began looking for space to replace the area that The Food Project already occupied.

Part of our research process was to investigate any laws that we could use to prolong our stay, and/or to be compensated for having to move and relocate. We eventually found several Zoning Laws that provided some protection in regard to having access to certain rights. Within our state of Massachusetts and also within our City of Lynn, there are Zoning Laws that essentially state, that if any "green space" (natural land) is used for development or taken over for some reason, they need to replace that space somewhere else. Typically, this happens whenever a new park is created, or you see many trees being planted, or there's an expansion of a current park or playground. Having just been a part of a community effort to upgrade several parks and playgrounds, there was no need to fulfill with replacing the land by fixing up another park or playground.

We put forth the effort to agree to relocate as soon as we had a designated area for us to start over. The land being occupied by The Food Project was being used as a small farm, so our move would have to meet the same (or more) space requirement. Rather than wait for local government to decide how and where the land should be replaced, we drafted plans for a small farm to help serve the community. This, along with the success of the Warren Park Community Garden (which is only about 2 city blocks down the street from Lynn Tech), created leverage by having a history of success needed to create what is now the Lynn Tech Farm located at Lynn Vocation Technical Institute High School in Lynn, MA.

Note:

Wherever you live, if you see land being used or developed on (even a small space) this signifies potential space that will be available for use unless there are already plans your local government has. If your local government does not yet have any specific plans for replacing the green space they are now occupying, this will help you bargain specifically for the land space you will want to use. Having finances in order and an attorney who specializes in land ownership, this is where you can seek out opportunities for purchasing the land pace you want to use (more details are explained later in this guide).

This was the last picture taken prior to construction.

After testing the soil and learning that it was contaminated enough that it would be hard to grow items here, we chose to lay down several tons of gravel (rocks) and place compost on top. This would help us shape our structure and stay within the guidelines of our plan for the farm when creating different size plots available for the community.

This was the final result after laying out the compost and building a few garden beds.

Here are some of the gardeners at our "Gardener's Day" event where everyone got to see their plot and break down some of the dirt that hardened somewhat from the end of the winter months just passing by. We worked together in teams helping one another break down the compost and dirt to prepare our plots for the growing season.

We simply added a layer of compost on top of each plot and began to break down the dirt. There was a lot of moisture held within the dirt which was vital for our plants as we began planting and transplanting into the soil.

Labeling each plot is a great way to introduce gardeners to their neighbors and also keep things organized. Names, plots, and overall management of the garden can be a lot, so labeling each gardener's plot will help save some time. This will also help everyone work together when discussing what they plan on growing. Certain foods grow much taller than others and you do not want one person's plot to shadow over another's as we want every plant that is in your growing space to flourish.

One of the final steps prior to installing a fence, was installing the water-drip irrigation system. The purpose of a drip irrigation system is to evenly water all plants regularly so that they get the amount of water they need, without overwatering or potentially having any plants dry out from not receiving enough water. We connected the drip irrigation to a main water pipeline connected to the school (Lynn Tech High School) where the drip irrigation would turn on whenever someone turned on the hose to water their plants. This way, every time someone would water their plants, everyone would benefit from it. During days we would receive more rain, all we would have to do is turn of the drip irrigation to avoid any plants from getting washed out. However, on hotter days, the drip irrigation fulfilled its role without everyone having to water their plants which helped to save a lot on water.

To Learn More In Depth about installing your own drip-irrigation system with videos to follow for instructions, scan the QR Code below

7 Process Of Purchasing Land For Ownership

More and more land is continuously being bought/sold. Unlike businesses, storefronts, and merchandise, more land will not be added to the Earth. Once it is all "bought" it will only be available for purchase from an owner for much more than it is worth.

Same process United States took to make a purchase for the Louisiana Territory ("Louisiana Purchase") and many other countries take for granting land ownership (not including the barbaric and ruthless mass genocide that was also included in that process of owning land). Identifying smaller portions of land available for purchase will follow these steps listed below.

First, here are two steps to take always take note of throughout your land purchasing process:

1. Make Sure The Land Is Suitable

An urban land parcel with no buildings on it is a great start for a community garden, but there are other characteristics that make a vacant lot good or not-so-good for growing greens.

Key Questions To Consider:

- Does the lot you're eyeing get a good amount of sun—six to eight hours per day?
- Is it relatively flat?
- Is it within walking distance of nearby homes?
- Does it have any debris in it that couldn't easily be moved by volunteers, like giant hunks of concrete or a rusted-out car? (If there is giant-size debris, you don't need to write off the lot

yet; just note that you'll have to enlist some additional muscle to move it, and might have to make special arrangements to dispose of it.)

2. Check Zoning Laws & Water Availability

In most cases, this won't be a problem, since the lot you want to garden on is likely in a residential or mixed-use area, and since local governments are increasingly aware of the benefits community gardening brings. But especially if there's any doubt, it doesn't hurt to look up the lot's address on your town's zoning map (many are online or are easy to locate in any local government office) to make sure that the district in question allows community gardens—or at least does not expressly prohibit them.

Water is the lifeblood of any garden, so definitely check into this step. Try to find out if a water source is available on the site you're interested in. If you can't find evidence of one and the owner isn't sure, contact your local water utility to ask if the property has a water meter. If they aren't sure, you can ask if they'll conduct a site investigation to find out. If your identified site has had water service in the past, it should be relatively inexpensive to get a new water meter installed (if you need one). If the site has never had water service, installing a line that connects to the street main could cost much more. Your water utility should be able to give you more info. As a last resort, you can work with a local business or storefront nearby to agree to serve as a water source (there are often "tax breaks" in it for them as incentives for being a water source for your community garden).

"Buy Land, they're not making it anymore" - Mark Twain

Finding land for sale in the United States can be difficult at times as many people will try to sell online and take advantage of people. Also, the pricing of certain land may not always match the investment you think you are making. Here are some steps to begin with when looking to identify land you wish to purchase.

Here Is A Step-By-Step Process To Follow When Buying Land

Step 1: Find Land For Sale

You won't always be lucky enough to drive past a plot of land that's the perfect investment opportunity for you.

If you know for certain you want to buy land, but don't have any specific property in mind yet, try doing an online search. A FREE online resource with many options and helpful information is LandWatch (www.landwatch.com). This resource has listings for land, farms, and ranches, hunting land, home properties, commercial land, and much more.

If you'd rather have help with sorting through all the possibilities for a match that fits your specific needs/interests, you can always speak to a Real Estate Agent. There may be many Real Estate Agents who live locally, but when planning for an investment, you want to speak to someone who specializes in land plots; this may come with a fee but is worth it in the long run. A helpful resource for finding someone who specializes in land plots can be found here: https://www.homelight.com/buying

Step 2: Dig Into The Smaller Details

The first thing you should look into is the Zoning Laws for the county. What are zoning laws? They're rules and regulations that local governments use to control how property is developed.

For example, if you're wanting to purchase (or sell off individual lots) you'll need to know if you're allowed to subdivide the land. You'll be able to find this information in either the city or county government offices.

The most common restrictions you'll find for zoning include:

- The type of buildings allowed
- A specific kind of business not allowed
- Size and height of buildings
- Location of utility lines

Once you know what restrictions are in place for the plot of land, you'll also want to look into whether permits come with the land. If you're wanting to build anything on the land, there are permit obligations you must attend to. You most often need permits for:

- **Sewer.** You'll need to know if there's enough sewer capacity for a connection to be made. If the property is far from the nearest sewer line, your best option might be to go with a private septic system.
- **Utilities.** If you need a public water hookup or access to the electrical grid, you'll also need permits for that.
- **Road access**. Different factors will affect how much it costs to pave a road through the land, or whether it'll be allowed at all. If the land is covered in trees, they'll need to be cleared first. If the land is near a conservation area or has endangered animals, construction work is often limited or outright restricted.

Finding useable land is a major issue. If a river goes through it or the land is nearby a lake or many trees, this is actually destroying the value of the land. This an ironic statement, but it costs about $700 to remove a tree to use land to develop on. Using the land for growing produce or turning into a farm or garden will have its own costs but deciding if a tree is going to block any sunlight so your farm or garden can remain successful can bring about additional costs.

Step 3: Get Your Funding And Financing In Order

Most options for purchasing land come down to the cash Offer that is submitted. A "Cash Offer" does not mean you can pay the entire amount up front as there are many purchasing options and financing options available.

You'll want to get some document in order when you are ready to make an offer.

1. First, the seller is likely to want to see proof of funds. Sellers want to see that you can cover down payment, closing costs, etc. Proof of funds should be on an official letterhead from the institution where your funds are. The date, name of the account holder, and the balance of funds should all be listed.Other examples of documentation for proof of funds that a seller might accept include a bank statement, a copy of a money market account balance, or an open equity line of credit.

Depending on the land type and request from the seller(s) you also want to have:

2. Pre-qualifying and Pre-approval letters from you bank. These letters are just a reflection of available amounts that you could afford given you are making a down-payment.

- Pre-qualifying just involves a credit check, so it is important to not make any additional expenses during this time even though this step is easily achieved and is simple to accomplish. You also want to make sure your credit is in good standing and have any outstanding balances and that everything is up to date.
- Pre-approval is the amount you are approved based on your income, down payment amount, and credit history. You can get as many pre-approvals as you request within a 30-day period. You do want to avoid getting numerous pre-approvals as it can hinder your credit, especially if it is outside of that 30-day window.

Step 4: Make an offer to the seller in writing

Verbal agreements are not solid agreements when purchasing land (or doing any other purchase or transaction). Any details that might affect the value of the land you wish to buy should be put down in writing immediately.

The most common type of contract used to make an offer is the real estate agent's "Bid Offer" form. You can find many samples of a Bid Offer online but, here's a Sample Bid Offer Form.

SAMPLE AGREEMENT TO PURCHASE REAL ESTATE (LAND)

The undersigned (herein "Purchaser") hereby offers to purchase from the owner (herein "Seller") the real estate located at ______________________in the city of______________________, County of_______________, State of_________________________, the legal description of which is:____________________________

_____________________ ____

____ ____________

____

____________ upon the following terms and conditions:

1. Purchase Price and Conditions of Payment The purchase price shall be ______________________________ __Dollars ($__________) to be paid in accordance with subparagraph_________________________, below:

A: Cash. The purchase price shall be paid in its entirety in cash at the time of closing the sale.

B: Cash Subject to New Mortgage. The purchase price shall be paid in cash at the time of closing the sale subject, however, to Purchaser's ability to obtain a first mortgage loan within __________days after the acceptance of this offer by Seller in the amount of $_____________, payable in not less than ____________ monthly installments, including interest at a rate not to exceed ____________% financing. If such financing cannot be obtained within the time specified above, then either Purchaser or Seller may terminate this agreement and any earnest money deposited by Purchaser will be promptly refunded.

C: Cash Subject to Existing Mortgage. The purchase price shall be paid in cash at the time of closing the sale after deducting from the purchase price the then outstanding balance due and owing under the existing mortgage in favor of ____________, dated____________, 20___, in the original amount of $______________; of such mortgage debt is approximately $_______________ as of _______________, 20____.

D: Cash With Assumption of Existing Mortgage. The purchase price shall be paid in cash at the time of the closing of the sale after deducting from the purchase price the then outstanding balance due and owing under the existing mortgage in favor of ______________, dated________________, 20___,having a present balance of approximately $_________________________, as of ______________, 20___, which the purchaser hereby assumes and agrees to pay in accordance with its terms and to perform all of its provisions; purchaser shall pay any and all payments coming due after the closing of the sale. Any transfer fees required by the mortgage shall be paid by______________.

E: Sale by Land Contract. The purchase price shall be paid in accordance with the certain land contract attached hereto and incorporated into this contract by this reference. The down payment to be made at the time of closing this sale shall be $____________and the balance of $___________shall be paid at the rate of __________% per annum.

2. Earnest Money Deposit As earnest money Purchaser deposits $_________________with the broker which shall be applied to the purchase price at the time of closing the sale. In the event that this offer is not accepted by Seller this earnest money deposit shall be promptly refunded to Purchaser by the broker. In the event that this offer is accepted by Seller and Purchaser shall fail to perform the terms of this agreement the earnest money deposit shall be forfeited as and for liquidated damages suffered by Seller. Seller is not, however, precluded from asserting any other legal or equitable remedy, which may be available to enforce this agreement.

3. Real Estate Taxes, Assessments, and Adjustments Real Estate Taxes accrued against the property shall be prorated through the date of closing the sale and Seller shall pay all taxes allocated to the

property through that date of acceptance of this offer to purchase. Rents, if any, shall be prorated through the date of closing and all rent deposits shall be transferred to Purchaser. Existing casualty insurance shall be canceled/prorated through the date of closing.

4. Title to the Property Seller shall provide purchaser prior to the closing and promptly after the acceptance of this offer, at Seller's expense and at Seller's option an abstract of title to the property brought down to date or an owner's policy of title insurance in an amount equal to the purchase price, said abstract of policy to show marketable or insurable title to the real estate in the name of Seller subject only to easements, zoning and restrictions of record and free and clear of all other liens and encumbrances except as stated in this offer. If the abstract or title policy fails to show marketable or insurable title in Seller a reasonable time shall be permitted to cure or correct defects. Seller shall convey title to Purchaser at the time of closing by a good and sufficient general warranty deed free and clear of all liens and encumbrances except as otherwise provided in this offer and subject to easements, zoning, and restrictions of record.

5. Possession of the Property Purchaser shall be given possession of the property on ________________, 20____. A failure on the part of Seller to transfer possession as specified will not make Seller a tenant of Purchaser, but in such event Seller shall pay to Purchaser $____________________per day as damages for breach of contract and not as rent. All other remedies, which Purchaser may have under law, are reserved to Purchaser.

6. Risk of Loss The risk of loss by destruction or damage to the property by fire or otherwise prior to the closing of the sale is that of Seller. If all or a substantial portion of the improvements on the property are destroyed or damaged prior to the closing and transfer of title this agreement shall be void able at Purchaser's option and in the event Purchaser elects to avoid this agreement the earnest money deposited shall be promptly refunded.

7. Improvements and Fixtures Included This offer to purchase includes all improvements, buildings and fixtures presently on the

real estate including but not limited to electrical, gas, heating, air conditioning, plumbing equipment, built-in appliances, hot water heaters, screens, storm windows, doors, Venetian blinds, drapery hardware, awnings, attached carpeting, radio, television antennas, trees, shrubs, flowers, fences and ____________________
____
____
____
____

8. General Conditions It is expressly agreed that this agreement to purchase real estate includes the entire agreement of Purchaser and Seller. This agreement shall be binding upon the heirs, personal representatives, successors and assigns of both Purchaser and Seller. This agreement shall be interpreted and enforced in accordance with the laws of the State of______________________
_______.

9. Special Conditions ____________________________________
____
____
____
____

10. Time for Acceptance and Closing This offer is void if not accepted by Seller in writing on or before ____________________ A.M./P.M. of the ______________________day of ________________________, 20____. Closing of the sale shall take place ____________ days after Purchaser's receipt of an abstract showing marketable title in Seller or title insurance binder showing insurable title in Seller. This offer is made at ______________________________, State of __________________, this ____________________ day of ___________________________, 20_______.

________________________ (PURCHASER)
____________________________ (PURCHASER) Acceptance by Seller The foregoing offer to purchase real estate is hereby accepted in accordance with the terms and conditions specified

above. The undersigned hereby agrees to pay a brokerage fee of $____________________ to ____________________, broker, in accordance with the existing listing contract. Dated this ________________ day of _______________, 20_____. ________________________ (SELLER) ________________________ (SELLER).

On the contract, you'll want to include the price of the land, its location or parcel number, as well as contingencies.

It's likely you'll still have a few lingering questions about the land when you make your offer. Contingencies are meant to **help protect you**. It's only after your offer is accepted that you'll want to invest time and money into answering certain questions.

Contingencies mean that if anything unsatisfactory turns up during the inspection period, you'll be able to back out of the deal and even get your earnest money back.

The most common contingencies for buying land with a cash offer include:

- That the land can pass an environmental test
- The land is able to get a septic system permit
- That there's an up-to-date survey that shows the correct boundaries and parcel size, as well as any possible easements or encroachments
- That the zoning regulations meet the buyer's needs

Once the offer is accepted, the next form you might use is a "Sales and Purchase Agreement (SPA). Both forms are legal, binding documents, however, in some states these two forms can be combined into one contract. You can then get locked into an obligation to buy under the seller's terms. So, if you aren't using a real estate agent, be sure to do your research and read over all paperwork with great care.

Step 5: Make Your Deposit

When you make your cash offer, you'll also include "earnest money". Earnest money is typically a small amount of money that goes into an escrow (funds held by a third party) to show you're a serious buyer. If you walk away from the deal for any reason not listed under the contingencies (this should illustrate how important it is you use contingencies to protect yourself), the seller gets to keep the money.

Step 6: Get Environmental Tests Done

When buying land, environmental testing is as important as getting a home inspection before you purchase.You want to know if the soil is contaminated. An environmental test can also tell you if there's earthquake damage or sinkhole possibilities.

Something else you'll want to look into is the moisture content of the soil. If you plan to build on the land, you'll want to ensure the ground is stable enough to support the structure you're planning. More importantly, soil may need to be replaced due to erosion or moisture issues. Depending on the size of land you are looking to purchase, this can come with a large price tag.

Step 7: Look Into A Land Survey

Once you have a land survey done, you'll know exactly where the boundaries are. Surveyors will mark the corners of the land with a rebar that lays flush with the ground. If they find any buried pipes, surveyors also use monument markers, such as a wood stake, to mark the location. This will help clarify how much you may pay in taxes or expenses that are not under your direct responsibility if someone owns land next to your space.

Doing a land survey will help you not misinterpret how much acreage you're actually buying. Certain parts of the land may not be useable. You may purchase 40 acres, but only 38 acres are useable.

Step 8: Check Over The Title

Just like with purchasing a house, liens can be placed on land for various reasons, such as outstanding taxes. Owners of the property want to receive what is owed to them, but so do the banks and/or credit unions.

Before you purchase the land, make sure the land has a clear title. A simple "Title Search" will cost you between $75 to $100, but is well worth the investment.

A Title Search can also determine whether there are any special assessments, restrictions, or easements on the property. Sometimes, a third party can have a right to use part of the property. This third party could be a utility company that has the right to install poles for power lines or oil company having right to work on pipelines that control and manage.

Step 9: Do Your Final Walkthrough

While you aren't actually always able to do a "walk-through" like one does when buying a home, you'll want to tour the land. Exploring the property on foot will not only help you understand the shape of the property, but will also give you a chance to confirm any findings from doing a land survey or title check.

As there are many available options when buying land over the internet, you do not want to be tricked or taken advantage of. Plan accordingly when preparing for this step.

Step 10: Get Ready To Pay

Once everything has met to your satisfaction during the inspection period, it's time to pay the seller.The most common method of payment in a cash deal is a cashier's check. Personal checks aren't acceptable when it comes to large amounts of money exchanging hands. A cashier's check helps to alleviate any concerns of legitimacy by having the funds issued by a bank.

Step 11: Completing Your Deal

After you've delivered the cashier's check, it's time to get your hands on the Deed. A Deed is a legal document that transfers property ownership from a seller/grantor to a buyer.

One option is to close at the registry office where you will record the deed. You can also choose to close at a title company.

If you don't have a real estate agent helping you through the process, you might want to consider hiring an attorney to look over the contracts for you first. In some states, the attorney can even handle filing the Deed for recording. A real estate agent who specializes in land deals will know how to protect your best interests in a contract.

Financing Options For Purchasing Land

These are not the ONLY financing options available

1. **Construction-to-permanent (CP) loan**. Also called a "combined construction". A CP loan allows the buyer to finance the land purchase and home/land construction simultaneously. It is the most common financing option because it often requires a smaller down payment, has a lower interest rate, and is offered by most lenders. Before applying for a CP loan, you will usually have to hire a licensed contractor and have building plans drafted. The lender often stipulates the maximum amount of time you can wait to begin construction.

2. **Lot loan.** Lot loans allow you to finance a land purchase without immediate plans to build on the property. Lot loans aren't offered by most lenders, who see them as riskier than construction loans and also require larger down payments and have higher interest rates.

3. **Owner financing.** On some properties, the seller may offer to finance the purchase directly. The required down payment will depend on the seller, but they're typically lower than conventional financing. The interest rates are usually higher with this option as well.

Buying Land: Pros

- The ability to do whatever you choose with the land: When you purchase land, you are free to do with it as you please, as long as it meets Zoning laws and regulations. Building on vacant land allows you to create your vision from start to finish, whether that vision is a farm, a property to generate revenue, or building the home of your dreams.

- Outright, Direct Ownership: Many vacant land purchases are made in cash, meaning that you will immediately own your investment outright. Even if you are able to finance raw land (land that has not been developed or currently ready for construction at time of purchase), you are more likely to pay it off in a much shorter time frame than you would a developed piece of land.

- Low Maintenance: Vacant land that is part of a buy-and-hold investment strategy may not require too much maintenance. Of course, the opposite could be true too. The trick is to buy vacant land you are comfortable maintaining.

- Affordability: Taxes and fees for vacant land are typically much lower than they would be on developed land, making vacant land cheaper to own over the long run. You may also get a deal when purchasing the land since many owners of vacant land are highly motivated sellers. These factors can make a huge impact on your long-term return on investment (ROI).

Buying Land: Cons

- More Difficult To Finance: How hard is it to get a loan to purchase land? Very. Without a structure in place to serve as collateral, banks and other financing institutions will typically loan a much lower percentage of value on underdeveloped land. You can help overcome this by presenting to your lender with a solid plan for developing land (if that is your intention) before you ask for financing. Otherwise, prepare yourself with a hefty down payment for any vacant land financing.

- Delayed Returns On Investment: Without rental income coming in, your land won't be making any money to cover expenses like property taxes or improvements to the land. If you cannot absorb these costs long-term, you may need to get creative to cover these types of expenses. You can rent out the land to seasonal businesses (pumpkin patches, Christmas Tree lots, etc) or other transitory businesses.

- You Cannot Claim Depreciation: Depreciation does not apply to underdeveloped land, which means you cannot claim this as a tax deduction like you would on developed land. Additionally, you won't have a mortgage, so you won't be able to deduct mortgage interest during tax season.

- The Land May Not Be Permitted (yet): Permitting can be a time-consuming and tedious process. Current zoning and permitting for a given piece of land is something you will find out during your due diligence, which means overcoming zoning and permitting issues will be a part of your plan from the very beginning. There has to be an understanding of what you want permitted, in addition to having the space you are developing, to be permitted during your process.

Purchasing land still often comes with fees, taxes, penalties, etc. To remove many potential financial barriers and owning a land outright, you can look into Land Acquisition. This may be one of the final ways of purchasing land in the world as more space is being bought by major companies and corporations.

What Should You Put On Vacant Land?

Part of learning how to purchase vacant land involves learning how to identify the best purpose for the land. Vacant land presents a blank slate for land use purposes. As an investor, you have many options for how you can use this space. Here are some ideas to keep in mind whether you purchase land or may be looking to invest in other opportunities:

1. Produce Farm

2. Wind Farm
3. Solar Energy
4. Vineyard
5. Golf Course
6. Event Rentals
7. Parking Lot
8. Sports Field
9. Concert Venue
10. Outdoor Advertising
11. Home Stables
12. Storage
13. Junkyard

**For the purposes of this book, purchasing land for the use of growing sustainable agriculture is best when planning for lifestyle and providing health for self. However, after your initial investment and working through your space when growing your own produce, it can be a plan to purchase additional land elsewhere or nearby for one (or more) of the ideas listed above.

Purchasing Land Example #1

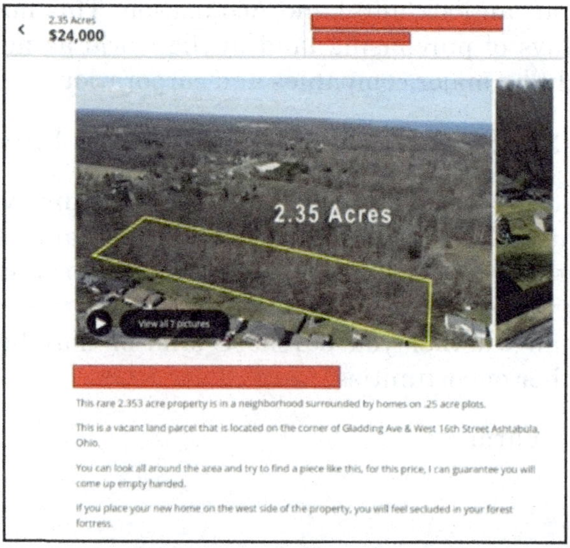

This is an example of a land property listing on www.landwatch.com. There are many pieces of land similar to this one, but this one stood out based on its location and potential. One thing to remain mindful of is not getting caught up with viewing a piece of land for sale that just looks nice, or has a really clear picture. You want to think of potential problems but also what offers you the least number of issues. The first thing you probably notice are the houses. This may intrigue you or deter you away if you were expecting an open lot in the middle of a field. What must always be examined is the potential the land provides; this most often is not overlooked by the seller(s).

Here are a few things to consider when viewing a land like the one in this listing:

1. Proximity To The Street – this may seem like an issue if you were planning for an open lot in a field somewhere. However, with an entire neighborhood right next door, this means that a water source and sewer system are already set in place, in addition to electricity. Having these resources nearby can help you get a jump start on any plans you may have wanted to begin with. Not having these resources nearby would create several barriers which would cost you more time and money.

2. Nearby To A University – a college or university may not come to mind as a selling point when looking to purchase land, but there are many benefits this can provide to help you space reach its' potential. This particular piece of land is close to Kent State University in Ohio. Having a large student population close by can help provide extra assistance and awareness of your growing space. Many students often looking for volunteer opportunities whereas others may be able to tie together volunteer work with their academic requirements based upon their field of study. Grants and funding are another resource that can be available when connecting with a college and/or university. Many schools will also pay students for completing volunteer work as well.

3. Ability to Finance – being located nearby homes and water/sewer systems makes this land a part of the town that would eventually become used for some form of development by the town, if not purchased by an individual or group of individuals. Having homes next door means that home equity is involved which would make Financing a viable option for this space as the estimates and value can be predetermined regardless of your plans. Financing can almost guarantee paying off the majority of the loan by also having multiple investors which would equal a lower interest rate. Connecting with local non-profits doing similar initiative can help get the community involved and also help create more interest in donating to efforts which will help complete the purchase of this land.

What To Do With 2.35 Acres Of Land?

There are 43,560 square feet per acre of land. If you're capable of producing 60,000lbs of food; that equates to almost 1.4 pounds of organic food per square foot. You are looking at approximately 130,000-135,000 pounds of food with 2.35 acres of land. This would mean you are using the land to its fullest potential during the growing season(s). If you refer back to the Lynn Tech Farm, I helped to establish in my community is slightly larger than ½ acre of land. With this space, we have regularly contributed to local Farmer's Markets where produce is for sale, and adding additional items to local CSA Boxes that are for sale within the community. This space takes a small group of individuals to manage along with each member taking care of their individual plot.

You would be able to fulfil many needs and grow many items with 2.35 acres of land.

Although 2.35 acres is enough land to build you dream home, building any larger-sized central meeting area can be a great investment. A large farmhouse, building, or even a storefront can be another idea for ways to maximize your space which will help keep everything organized will be a great investment.

Setting up rows would be ideal as you will have the space and area to determine where you want to grow each item based on sunlight and quantity. You could also make several garden beds to maximize space while keeping your growing areas neat and clean while preventing weeds from spreading.

Paying Off Investment

$24,000 can be split multiple ways.

Could be a challenge to find 24 people to invest $1,000 each but then everyone has equal ownership (or at least will feel like they do).

5 people would be a solid goal which would mean about $4,800/ each. Monthly payments of $400/month would pay off this land in one calendar year.

10 people would be able to pay off this land for about $200/month for one calendar year; or perhaps 5 people commit to $200/month for two calendar years.

5 people (plus donations)

- You may be able to create some fundraising, have a few people donate to your efforts from various online options available and have a goal of raising $5,000 (most people create a Go Fund Me for much more than that – note: Go fund Me will take about 10% of money raised so your listed goal will aim to be higher). Although you have to give back a percentage of the proceeds, you can attract many out-of-state investors and those who are willing to donate to your cause.
- Seeking produce and providing local CSA Boxes available to the community and local businesses should see a significant profit as well which can also be put towards paying off your land purchase.
- If this $5,000 goal is reached, then only $19,000 is left. Split between 5 people would equal $3,800/each) and a monthly payment of $316 for one year or $158 for two years.

Having 10 people who are willing to donate to pay off this land would equal (over two years) just $100/month. This would be to pay off this land outright. Many options are available while paying of the land that can happen such as building on it, growing foods, and other fundraising activities that will help cut costs over time.

Most often an initial investor will contribute more, or a few investors will be able to pay off their share from the beginning. No matter how the land is eventually paid off, you can start working on plans immediately after being granted owner of this space. Paying off the land will simply allow you to have one less payment to be accountable for. There will still be property and land taxes, but these can be paid off by continuous fundraising efforts and/or contributions from investors.

Anytime there's a purchase of land, you want to pay it off as soon as possible but, don't be in a rush either. As you can get to work on creating your plans for your land, you don't want all of your money tied up into just paying off the land. You can pay it off as you go and continuc to draft and add to plans you want for your space.

Purchasing Land Example #2

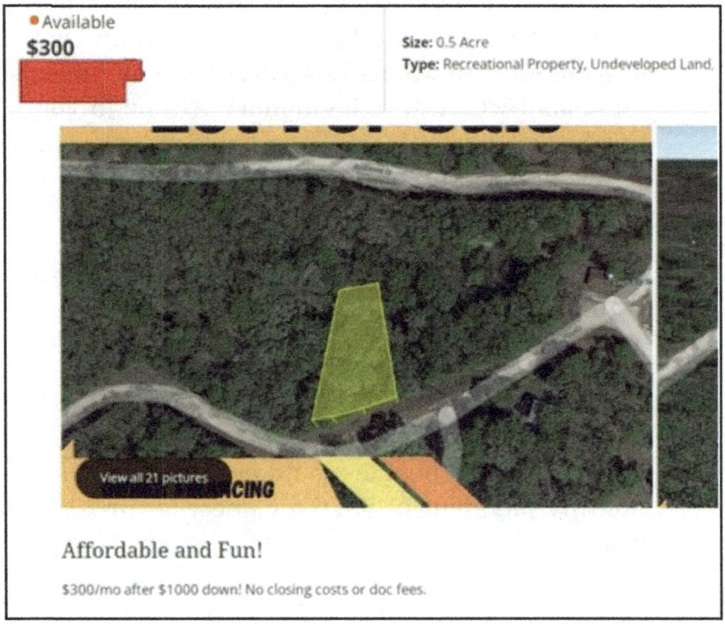

This piece of land costs $300/month for a total cost of $7000 (or 4,841 if paid in fullwith cash). Just following the projected monthly payment this land will be paid off within two calendar years. With a discounted cash price, this should leave room for negotiation with the seller. The seller has in their listing that the buyer cannot build until the land is paid off. Although this may seem to halt any plans you may have or feel eager to start with, it can help you long term with this option.

First, you can commit to just paying your monthly payment (with no additional expenses) and you use your time to plan out what exactly you want to do with your land once it's paid off. Putting together resources and planning ahead can help you save time long-term, as opposed to making a down payment and moving too fast with your plans.

This more affordable option will provide you with experience of owning land while having the necessary time to work through any barriers or challenges that you may encounter. Having a smaller piece of land is a great investment tool for not only getting started with owning land, but with having access to resources and helpful tools that can teach you more about land ownership if you choose to sell land in the future.

The land of this space is slightly smaller than the land at the Lynn Tech Farm in Chapter 6 if you want a picture view for a reference point of what you can grow within that space.

Purchasing Land Example #3 (Auction)

Many areas of land remain unclaimed and go on sale for auction. Many times, sellers just want to sell their land due to not being able to complete plans they initially had, or just want to cut their losses. Large areas of land are often bought by banks and then sold at action for those interested.

Although auctions are not the most feasible for knowing what you're exactly getting with your purchase, they can be an investment for you to pay lower than anticipated for the amount of land. The risk, however, is that there may be many barriers or issues that go unnoticed or were never explored. You will also want to do your due diligence if purchasing land through an auction. Don't get caught up in being able to purchase many acres of land for a lower-than-expected price, as the potential barriers may outweigh the benefits of owning a large area of land.

On the other hand, an auction can be the prime location for gaining access to large land area that you can own and have an enormous amount of room for plans you may have.

*You may also divide the land bought on auction and sell it too if you're looking to make a quick profit.

8 The Homestead Act of 1862, Zoning Laws, and Ordinances

The Homestead Act of 1862

President Abraham Lincoln signed the Homestead Act on May 20, 1862. On January 1, 1863, Daniel Freeman (American Homestead, U.S. Army Scout, and Civil War Veteran) made the first claim under the Act, which gave citizens or future citizens up to 160 acres of public land provided they live on it, improve it, and pay a small registration fee. The Government granted more than 270 million acres of land while the law was in effect.

The distribution of Government lands had been an issue since the Revolutionary War. At the time of the Articles of Confederation, the major controversy related to ownership was, land measurement and pricing. Early methods for allocating unsettled land outside the original 13 colonies were arbitrary and chaotic. Boundaries were established by stepping off plots from geographical landmarks. As a result, overlapping claims and border disputes were common. Land that was seized through force from citizens was not often granted by government as land ownership which created additional conflict and unrest within the country outside of the 13 colonies.

The Land Ordinance of 1785 finally implemented a standardized system of land ownership that eased boundary conflicts. Using astronomical starting points, territory was divided into a 6-mile square called a "township". A"township" was divided into 36 sections, each measuring one square mile or 640 acres each. Sale of public land was viewed as a means to generate revenue for the Government rather than as a way to encourage settlement at this time. Initially, an individual was required to purchase a full section of land at the cost of $1 per acre for 640 acres. The investment needed to purchase these large plots and the massive amount of physical labor required to clear the land for agriculture were often insurmountable obstacles. Due to these large tasks, smaller pieces of land were for sale and laws were flexible.

By 1800, the minimum lot was halved to 320 acres, and settlers were allowed to pay in 4 installments, but prices remained fixed at $1.25 an acre until 1854. That year, federal legislation enacted that land prices had to reflect the desirability of the lot. Lots that had been on the market for 30 years, for example, were reduced to 12 ½ cents per acre, while other areas increased their cost. Soon after, extraordinary bonuses were extended to veterans and those interested in settling the Oregon Territory, making homesteading a viable option for some.

Before and after the Mexican-AmericanWar in the mid-1800s, there was immense pressure to change policies,from the evolving economyto new/changing demographics, to the shifting social climate in 19th-century America. In the 1830s and 1840s, rising prices for corn, wheat, and cotton enabled large, well-financed farms, particularly the plantations of the South, to force out smaller ventures. Displaced farmers then looked westward to unforested country that offered more affordable development.

Prior to the war with Mexico (1846–48), people settling in the West demanded "preemption," an individual's right to settle land first and pay later (essentially an early form of credit). Eastern economic interests opposed this policy as it was feared that the cheap labor base for the factories would be drained, or that many would not be able to fulfil their promise to pay later. After the war with Mexico, a number of developments supported the growth of the homestead movement. Economic prosperity drew unprecedented numbers of immigrants to America, many of whom also looked westward for a new life. New canals and roadways reduced western dependence on the harbor in New Orleans, and England's repeal of its agricultural laws opened new markets to American agriculture.

Despite these developments, legislative efforts to improve homesteading laws faced opposition on multiple fronts. As mentioned above, Northern factories owners feared a mass departure of their cheap labor force and Southern states worried that rapid settlement of western territories would give rise to new states populated by small farmers opposed to slavery. Preemption became national policy in spite of these concerns. Three times—in 1852, 1854, and 1859—the House of Representatives passed homestead legislation, but on each occasion, the Senate defeated the measure. In 1860, a homestead bill providing Federal land grants to western settlers was passed by Congress only to be vetoed by President Buchanan.

Finally, in 1862, the Homestead Act was passed and signed into law. The new law established a three-fold homestead acquisition process: (1) file an application, (2) improve the land, and (3) file for deed of title.

Any U.S. citizen, or intended citizen, who had never borne arms against the U.S. Government could file an application and lay claim to 160 acres of surveyed Government land. For the next 5 years, the General Land Office looked for a good faith effort by the homesteaders. This meant that the homestead was their primary residence and that they made improvements upon the land. After 5 years, the homesteader could file for his patent (or deed of title) by submitting proof of residency and the required improvements to a local land office. If there were no improvements upon the land, or it was determined that their land was not their primary residence, granting ownership of the land was denied, but could be appealed in court.

Local land offices handling a deed for the title of the land would forward necessary paperwork to the General Land Office in Washington, DC, along with a final certificate of eligibility. The case file would then be examined, and valid claims were granted patent to the land free and clear, except for a small registration fee. Title could also be acquired after a 6-month residency and trivial improvements, provided the claimant paid the government $1.25 per acre. After the Civil War, Union soldiers could deduct the time they served from the residency requirements.

Some land speculators took advantage of legislative loopholes.

Others hired phony claimants or bought abandoned land. The General Land Office was underfunded and unable to hire a sufficient number of investigators for its widely scattered local offices. As a result, overworked and underpaid investigators were often susceptible to bribery.

Physical conditions on the frontier presented even greater challenges. Wind, blizzards, and plagues of insects threatened crops. Open plains meant few trees for building, forcing many to build homes out of sod. Limited fuel and water supplies could turn simple cooking and heating chores into difficult trials. While 160 acres may have been sufficient for an eastern farmer, it was simply not enough to sustain agriculture on the dry plains, and scarce natural vegetation made raising livestock on the prairie difficult. As a result, in many areas, the original homesteader did not stay on the land long enough to fulfill the claim.

Homesteaders who persevered were rewarded with opportunities as rapid changes in transportation eased some of the hardships. Six months after the Homestead Act was passed, the Railroad Act was signed, and by May 1869, a transcontinental railroad stretched across the frontier. The new railroads provided relatively easy transportation for homesteaders, and new immigrants were lured westward by railroad companies eager to sell off excess land at inflated prices. The new rail lines provided ready access to manufactured goods and catalog houses like Montgomery Ward offered farm tools, barbed wire, linens, weapons, and even houses delivered via the rails.

The distribution of western land by the Federal Government cannot be extricated from Federal Indian policy. The period from 1870 to 1900 marked a departure from earlier policies that were dominated by removal, treaties, reservations, and even war. New policy in the late 1880s – after the number of public lands available had rapidly diminished – focused specifically on breaking up reservations by granting land allotments to individual Native Americans. Seeking to satisfy the nation's hunger for land, Congress passed the Dawes Act in 1887, giving individual farms to Native American reservations and opening the remaining native American lands to settlers; land given to settlers became land Native Americans fought for via eminent domain as this land was theirs they had established, which was nullified due to regular construction of oil dwellings and railroads constructed going through their occupied land.

On January 1, 1863, Daniel Freeman and 417 others had filed claims. Many more pioneers followed, populating the land, building towns and schools, and creating new states from the territories. In many cases, the schools became the focal point for community life, serving as churches, polling places and social gathering locations.

In 1936, the Department of the Interior recognized Daniel Freeman as the first claimant and established the Homestead National Monument, near a school built in 1872, on his homestead near Beatrice, Nebraska. Today, the monument is administered by the National Park Service, and the site commemorates the changes to the land and the nation brought about by the Homestead Act of 1862.

By 1934, over 1.6 million homestead applications were processed and more than 270 million acres—10 percent of all U.S. lands—passed into the hands of individuals. The passage of the Federal Land Policy and Management Act of 1976 repealed the Homestead Act in the 48 contiguous states, but it did grant a ten-year extension on claims in Alaska.

**Although the Homestead Act has since ended, there are still areas of land that can be claimed if taken care of. Midwest states such as Kansas, Minnesota, Iowa, and Nebraska have land in small towns available as long as you follow certain guidelines. These states with land may ask that your home only be a certain size and fit within the parameters of the space you have. Start up costs for building a home, doing renovations, and maintaining your land can be costly but, it is an investment if you are planning to homestead long-term.

Zoning Laws & Ordinances

Many cities and towns have certain Zoning Laws that are to be taken advantage of when it comes to using public (or private) space for creating a growing space. Although many states are different, we will go over where I'm from (Massachusetts) to review in detail how certain Zoning Laws come into effect when getting space to grow items. You can then compare and contrast then to the state you live in.

States create Zoning Laws, bylaws, and ordinances to help promote desired patterns of development. The best interest of the community is not always on display with how they are written, but what they have in common is structure to work within which include specific use of space; more specifically, residential, commercial, industrial, and open space. Some communities allow mixed-use zones where they can provide a combination of the spaces listed.

Zoning Laws usually establish requirements for minimum lot size, street frontage, density, open space, parking, and the process for site plan approval. Certain uses are permitted as a matter of right, whereas others require a special permit. The concept of zoning is to promote public health, safety, and welfare, while encouraging the most appropriate use of land throughout the municipality. Zoning is a mechanism that allows communities to shape their own future. **It is essentially the single most powerful land use management tool we have at our disposal.** Creative Zoning regulations and bylaws/ordinances should allow for development that meets the community's economic and housing needs, while protecting natural resources. Zoning can contribute to, or help discourage plans within a community. Zoning should reflect and be responsive to different communities' needs and interests. Some communities will want to retain natural resources and agriculture, while others will want to promote commerce and industry. This is the importance of gathering resources and voices within the community, (even if it's a small portion of the community as a whole) because Zoning will appeal and back those who have some plan and interest in improving a space within the community.

Note: All changes to Zoning Laws must confirm to state Zoning standards and be approved by thecommunity's legislative body.

Massachusetts Zoning

Massachusetts is not the ideal location when you think of growing produce. However, I've been able to grow much produce here over the years, create Green Spaces relatively easier than most places, as Massachusetts does allow significant Zoning Laws that benefit those wanting to create their own growing space and flexibility.

The Massachusetts Subdivision Control Act (MGL Ch. 41 §81K-81GG) requires minimum frontage for the division of land into buildable lots and gives local planning boards authority over subdivision of land. Conventional local subdivision regulations do not address ecological values, public access, or other public amenities; they are established simply to regulate the laying out of new roads and lots. This often results in "cookie cutter" layouts and plans rather than tailoring themselves to meet a community's needs and/or interest. This is yet another reason how Zoning Laws can be taken advantage of by setting forth your plans that fit within a certain geographic area (as you're essentially doing their work for them) which can help move you closer to being granted approval.

If a proposed area meets the basic area/frontage requirements, the planning board must accept the lot through the "Approval Not Required" (ANR) guidelines. If not approved, specific layout plans must be proposed and recommended which you can use for re-submitting your proposal with the necessary corrections.

Open Space Zoning

The most popular layout of Open Space Zoning is, Open Space Residential Design (OSDR), which includes a four-step process that precedes formal planning board review:

1. Identify and set aside for protection critical natural habitat and/or other features such as buffers. That separate natural land and land for public use.

2. Identify appropriate sites for the homes or businesses
3. Locate roadways and other infrastructure
4. Draw in the low lines

These four steps allow communities to meet their housing needs without destroying natural resources. Homeowners receive added benefits of shared open space.

The Green Neighborhood Alliance force by the Mass Audubon (and several other groups) has developed model OSRD bylaws and regulations that are being utilized successfully by many communities. They have created numerous spaces to help preserve land space and maximize their potential by encouraging community output. Communities that wish to create their own growing spaces have been met with support and have been able to work collaboratively to maximize their vision.

Note: Due to communities having certain zones (percentagewise) established for open space, communities (or individuals) that develop plans for using this space to create initiatives such as a community garden, allows these same communities to develop in other areas things like businesses, condos, or other establishments. Although this can seem like a draw-back, being able to create a growing space is very necessary, especially in areas known as "food deserts" where this land would not be put to use, and local development could still find loopholes to establish their development plans.

Creative Zoning Models For The Future

Mixed-Use Zoning

Not particularly "new" but not all communities have adopted these forms of zoning as of yet (2021). These zones are modeled after traditional New England villages that had shops, homes, and small service providers all located within walking distance of on another, allowing a mixture of compatible uses in one geographic area. Mixed-use zoning can encourage village-style developments where residences and businesses share space and open space is left intact or public use.

Concentrated Growth Districts

Districts where relatively dense development is allowed can be used to encourage concentrated development around existing downtowns or other locations where infrastructure is available, and the land is appropriate for intensive development. This balances districts with less concentrated uses in locations that are more sensitive.

Performance Zoning

With performance zoning, restriction is placed on the impacts caused by a development, rather than on the categories of use. In this way, flexibility can be encouraged while affording maximal protection to the resources of concern. Examples include amount of traffic generated or the percentage of impervious surfaces allowed.

Conservation-Oriented Special Zoning, or Overlay District

Increased protection is provided for special categories of resources, such as floodplains, wetlands, riverfront areas, areas overlying water supplies, and historically significant areas. These protections can "overlay" (on top of or in addition to) the existing, "underlying" zoning, hence the term "Overlay District." In some cases, a conservation-oriented underlying district approach can be used, for example zoning areas with prime agricultural soils for agricultural use.

Low Impact Development (LID)

Low Impact Development addresses stormwater through small, cost-effective, landscape features located throughout the development instead of collecting water from large portions of a site and piping it to centralized retention/detention basins. LID helps replicate and retain the natural ways that rainfall is managed and distributed. It can be applied to new development as well as redevelopment and revitalization projects.

Transferable Development Rights (TDRs)

Landowners in an area within a municipality targeted for preservation can agree to "sell" their development rights to landowners in areas that are more suitable for development. This is a relatively new tool that is currently being used in several Massachusetts communities, including Plymouth and Groton.

For more information on TDRs here: https://plannersweb.com/1998/07/putting-growth-in-its-place-with-transfer-of-development-rights/

Phased Growth and Building Moratoria

Communities experiencing rapid, unplanned, uncontrolled growth that threatens to overwhelm municipal services and degrade important aspects of the local environment and quality of life can limit the number of building permits issued each year to "phase their growth" based on infrastructure capacities or to avoid excessive growth while a community is in the process of updating its master plan and zoning.

Other communities may adopt a Building Moratorium to temporarily halt the issuance of new building permits or subdivision approval. Moratoria are not meant to stop development altogether but rather to give the community time to plan and improve standards to guide growth and development. However, beware: a moratorium can backfire if developers rush to get projects approved before the moratorium goes into effect. Careful attention is also needed in adopting such bylaws and ordinances in order to ensure that they are able to withstand court challenge. It is best if a community puts such a requirement in place for a specific period of time while needed capital facilities or infrastructure is being developed.

Occasionally, communities limit new connections to water or sewer systems because of inadequate supplies or capacities or they are to be ordered to do so by the state Department of Environmental Protection (DEP). If on-site water and septic are available, this may have little impact on overall growth.

Use Zoning Laws To Protect Environment

The following is an excerpt from Chapter 3 of Prof. John R. Nolon's new book, Protecting the Environment through Land Use Law: Standing Ground:

"Municipalities across the nation are incorporating natural resource preservation principles into their zoning ordinances. They are not doing so uniformly, but their collective progress is impressive. Some local legislatures describe the protection of the natural environment as a specific purpose of zoning. Localities may protect open space in zoning districts by adjusting applicable density, lot size, and setback restrictions. For example, conservation zoning districts permit only private land uses that are compatible with the natural environment, while agricultural zoning districts preserve agricultural land for farming purposes and open space.

Municipalities in several states have identified environmental protection as a purpose or goal of their zoning regulations. A purpose of the Durham County, North Carolina, zoning ordinance, for example, is to promote the health, safety, and general welfare of the residents of the city and county by conserving land and water resources, providing adequate light and air, and preventing overcrowding of land and undue concentrations of population. The zoning ordinance of the city of Manhattan, Kansas, includes in its statement of purpose a specific reference to the conservation of natural resources, including open space preservation.

In Pennsylvania, the township of West Manchester amended its single-family residential district regulations to require open space preservation in undeveloped areas. Before amending the ordinance, the local legislature prepared maps showing potential future development under the existing conventional zoning. This exercise, often described as a "build-out analysis," illustrated the great amount of existing open space and farmland that would be lost under the present zoning ordinance. In addition, the legislature mapped anticipated open space preservation to show landowners and developers exactly what was envisioned: interconnected open spaces crossing parcel lines.

In Santa Monica, California, one of the purposes of the zoning regulation is to protect and enhance the quality of the natural and built environment, and to ensure adequate park and public open space. Each of the city's zoning districts has certain property development standards. These standards include maximum unit density, lot coverage, building height, minimum lot size, setback requirements, and building spacing, as well as a requirement for open space. For example, in the Ocean Park residential zoning district there is a requirement that at least one hundred square feet per housing unit of usable common open space [be] accessible and available to all project residents for outdoor activities. Development in any of the city's residential districts must provide "usable" common open space, private open space, or both.

The zoning regulations of the town of Wallingford, Connecticut, require that existing trees are to be preserved to the maximum extent possible. Trees and landscaping are to be preserved and provided under the town's regulations to reduce excessive heat, glare, and accumulation of dust; to provide privacy from noise and visual intrusion; and to prevent the erosion of the soil, excessive run-off of drainage water, and the consequent depletion of the ground water table and the pollution of water bodies.

Conservation district zoning is used to carry out local environmental objectives. In Cumberland, Maryland, the Conservation District regulations provide that "no structure shall be erected, nor shall any material or equipment be stored, nor shall any fill be placed, nor shall the elevation of any land be substantially changed" except for certain permitted uses. These include agricultural, horticultural, and forestry uses; public and private parks; recreation areas; historic areas; conservation areas; and other similar uses employing open land with open structures, gardening, and outdoor plant nurseries. All residential uses are prohibited in the zoning district.

In Cheltenham Township, Pennsylvania, a Soil Conservation overlay district was created to protect steep slopes from inappropriate development and excessive grading, and to permit and encourage the use of these areas for open space purposes. Among the many objectives of this regulation is to "permit only those uses in steep slope areas that are compatible with the preservation of existing natural features . . . by restricting the grading of steep slope areas," and to protect individuals and adjacent landowners in the township from the possible harmful effects of inappropriate grading and development on steep slopes. Permitted uses in this zoning district are limited to passive recreational activities, wildlife sanctuaries, game farms, pastures, crop cultivation, and related uses. In Wells, Maine, a coastal community, a Resource Protection District was created to protect and preserve fragile environmental areas from intrusions that would upset ecological systems, or create potential public health or safety problems. Passive recreation is a permitted use in the district, while aquaculture, municipal facilities, piers, docks, and wharves are also permitted, subject to site plan approval.

The court upheld a legislative zoning change that applied to a single parcel in *Bartram v. Zoning Commission of City of Bridgeport* (68 A.2d 308, Conn. 1949). The parcel in question was limited to residential use. The owner sought to build a drug store, hardware store, grocery store, bakeshop, and beauty parlor in a residential neighborhood removed from the nearest shopping district. The amendment was granted, challenged by the neighbors, and invalidated by the trial court. On appeal, the Connecticut Supreme Court held that the rezoning was valid, noting that the means of achieving the purposes of zoning are within the discretion of the zoning authority and not subject to review of the courts unless the authority abused its discretion; a court is without authority to substitute its own judgment for that vested by the statutes in a zoning authority.

The zoning change in the 1949 Bartram decision was innovative for its time. To alleviate downtown traffic congestion, the city council decided to allow more services and retail products in small shopping centers in residential neighborhoods, much to the displeasure of nearby homeowners. By providing local goods and services, the neighborhood became more walkable, vehicle trips and vehicle miles traveled were reduced, and air quality in the downtown improved. In today's environment, we see such a zoning change as mitigating climate change by reducing greenhouse gas emissions, approximately 80% of which is carbon dioxide. Adjusting zoning to the realities of global warming and climate variation to mitigate its effects and adapt to its consequences is driving many zoning amendments in coastal and urban communities."

Purchase book here: https://www.eli.org/eli-press-books/protecting-environment-through-land-use-law-standing-ground

The Tree That Owns Itself

You may have seen this online as many people have shared their fascination and thoughts on this. What you are actually looking at is Zoning Laws and ownership working directly for the benefit of the owner(s) themselves.

Between 1820 and 1832, a man named Colonel William H. Jackson, a Professor at the University of Georgia, owned a small piece of land where the tree rests. Colonel Jackson loved the tree so much that he deeded it to the 8ft x 8ft plot of land that it was growing on.

According to local newspaper stories, few people of that time period knew of this tree ownership or knowledge of those who witnessed the original deed that Jackson drew up. So, there is question whether this deed ever existed. Many believe that the 1890 Weekly Banner article about the tree popularized the story so much, that the people living in the area of Athens, Georgia decided to go along with it, allowing the tree to own the square of land that it grows on.

The Tree That Owns Itself is a white oak tree that is believed to have first sprouted sometime between the mid-1500s and the late 1700s. when Athens, Georgia was formed, this tree was considered to be the largest tree in town – well over 100 feet tall. The tree flourished throughout the 19th century, but by 1906 this tree was struggling due to erosion. Erosion around the base of the tree was noticed by George Foster Peabody (American Banker and Philanthropist from Columbus, Georgia) who paid for the restoration and preservation work. Soil was replaced around the tree and erected the tablet that rests on the site today as well as a chain barricade supported by granite pillars around the tree.

About a year later, in 1907, the tree was damaged in an ice storm. Despite the community's efforts to preserve this tree, rot appeared, and the tree started to weaken. On October 9, 1942, the tree finally fell down.

The Son of the Tree That Owns Itself

While the original tree was gone, the community in Athens, Georgia loved the tree so much that several gardens in the area took acorns from it and spouted saplings. The plot on which the original tree once stood remined empty for four years until it was suggested that the Athens' Junior Ladies Garden Club do something about it.

One of the saplings grown from the original tree's acorns was chosen – a five-foot-tall specimen that the garden club agreed would have the best chance of survival. The University of Georgia College of Agriculture oversaw the planting of the new tree, and on December 4, 1946, mayor Robert L. McWhorter conducted an official dedication ceremony for the Son of the Tree That Owns Itself.

Since the time of being planted, the Son of the Tree That Owns Itself has flourished. Today, this tree still stands on the same land it inherited from its parent and has grown over 50 feet tall.

Today, there is a weathered stone marker which says the following words:

For and in consideration of the great love I bear this tree and the great desire I have for its protection for all time, I convey entire possession of itself and all land within eight feet of the tree on all sides.

The Tree That Owns Itself and the Son of the Tree That Owns Itself provides a scenario where Zoning Laws and ownership blend together in benefit of the owner. Although it is uncertain if the Tree(s) truly owned themselves, but with community support, ownership was agreed upon. Many laws work in a similar fashion which provide "loopholes" that are determined based upon what is required. In some states, local government may not require many documents for ownership whereas other states may require many parties to be involved which can prolong and complicate the ownership process. Regardless of which states you are in, you want to be aware of each step and not rush the process and end up potentially losing access to you land based on a technicality of some sort. While many choose to view in opposition of legal processes, there are many rights and laws in place to protect you and your investment that are provided at a State Level, Federal Level, and at a National Level that we can use to our advantage and benefit.

9 Introduction To Land Acquisition

Land acquisition means the process whereby a person is compelled by a public agency to alienate all or part of the land he or she owns or possesses to the ownership and possession of that agency, for public purpose, in return for a compensation. This process is mostly completed by large corporations and companies that plan to develop land for real estate or business. In countries like India, Land Acquisition is the power of a union or the state government to acquire private land for the purpose of industrialization, development of infrastructural facilities or "urbanization" of the private land, and to compensate the affected landowners for their rehabilitation and resettlement.

Within the United States "Land Acquisition" is outlines under the "Law of Compulsory Purchase".

United States (United Kingdom and Ireland): Law of Compulsory Purchase

Overseas (India): Land Acquisition (LARR ACT, 2013)

Law of Compulsory Purchase

The *Law of Compulsory Purchase* is, the process by which land is legally acquired for public use, irrespective of the wishes of the owner. This means that a buyer of the land can alter the land and its layout at their own discretion. A landowner may wish to keep the land as is to help preserve land, but a buyer may want to build a home or create an outlet mall in its place. The land is still purchased legally, but the wish of the owner is just not fulfilled; same is true for other land purchases.

The Law of Compulsory Purchase identifies a need for using your space for some type of development or plan that benefits the community. To follow along with the purpose of this book, buying land to use as a produce farm or creating some type of garden, will fall under this criteria. Future developments may happen such as plans to install a highway, oil or water pipeline, or other developmental site in which, you will be notified and can use your current landownership to sell and relocate, expand to another area, or be financially compensated without having to lose your space with nothing in return. As much as we may want to purchase land for our own individual plans, planning for future sale of your land is a part of the landownership process that should not be ignored.

Note: Although uncommon, some buyers will create plans such as building a highway and after you sell your land, they go with another plan such as housing, or building businesses. Although they are not being truthful, what is written in contract is considered to be the truth during negotiations. Once they are the new owners, they can do with the land as they please. This is why it is important that you view your landownership as an investment, as your intention and plans can and should be willing to change if necessary.

There are two procedures under which Compulsory Purchase may be achieved.

1 Involves the service of a **notice to treat** (compensation on the basis of the market value of the land at the date of the notice).

2 Through a **general *vesting declaration*** by the acquiring authority, as a result of which the land vests in the authority from the date of the declaration.

Compulsory Purchase Orders (CPO's) allow public bodies to force homeowners to sell if their property obstructs a regeneration project or it's for the "greater public good".

Standard Timeline Of Being Granted Compulsory Purchase Order (CPO) (using the year (2021) this book has been published)

January 2021	**Information Gathering and Preparation of CPO Draft Documents**	Acquiring authority drafts the CPO, CPO Plan, schedule of interests, and statement of reasons. Prepares a report to the relevant authorizing committee.
February 2021	**Report To Committee and Resolution To Use CPO Powers**	Acquiring authorities will require a detailed report on the proposed use of compulsory purchase powers in order to authorize the use of those powers.
February 2021	**Serve "Requisition For Information" notices**	The acquiring authority will serve notice on all people they believe own or occupy the land they wish to acquire. The requisition for information notice usually specifies a deadline of 21 days for response although it can take longer to gather all the information required.
March 2021	**Acquiring Authority Make CPO**	Once all of the information for acquiring landownership is collected, the acquiring authority makes the CPO and serves notice of it on parties with "qualifying interests". The acquiring authority put up site notices and publishes in local newspapers as well. The CPO, CPO Plan and statement of reasons are made available for inspection.
April 2021	**Statutory Period For Objections**	The period for objectives will be set out in the notice and is a minimum of 21 days from the date notice is served, displayed, or first published. Objectives must be in writing. If there are other orders required, the objection period may be longer.

May 2021	**Objections Received**	Where relevant objectives are received, the Secretary of State will order a public local inquiry into the CPO. Objections to level of compensation payable will not be considered. Where no objections are received (or objections are resolved), the CPO can be confirmed without the need for an inquiry.
June 2021	**Secretary Of State Issues "Relevant Date" Letter**	The relevant date letter sets the official date for the inquiry and sets out the deadline for the acquiring authority to serve its' statement of case.
July 2021	**Deadline For Lodging "Statement Of Case" For Public Local Inquiry**	The deadline for lodging the statement of case will usually be 6 weeks after the date of the "relevant date" letter. Remaining objectors may also be asked to provide a statement of case prior to the inquiry.
October 2021	**Inquiry And Site Visit**	The inquiry is normally held 22 weeks after the relevant date. The date will depend on the duration of the inquiry and the availability of an inspector. An inspector will hear evidence from the acquiring authority and the remaining objectors. A pre-inquiry meeting may also be held. The inspector will usually visit the site. There are procedures for both, accompanied and unaccompanied site visits.
November 2021	**Inspector's Report**	The inspector to the inquiry issues their written report, setting out conclusions and recommendations for consideration by the Secretary of State.
February 2022	**Secretary of State Decision**	After considering the inspector's report, the Secretary of State issues a decision to either confirm, modify, or reject the CPO. The decision letter sets out their

		reasons for their decision and is sent to the acquiring authority and any remaining objectors and anyone eels who requested notification.
March 2022	**CPO Confirmed**	Acquiring authority publicizes their decision in local media outlets as soon as possible after receipt of decision letter.
April 2022	**Judicial Review Challenge Period**	The validity of a CPO can be challenged during this period. This time period is within 6 weeks of the date of the first publicized notice.
July 2022	**Implementation of CPO**	The CPO can be implemented, and land is then acquired following publication. This process usually takes about 3 months.

**Upon being granted a CPO, you will also need (1) A schedule of properties affected (if any) and (2) A detailed map of the land you plan to purchase.

Emanate Domain Protection

Property rights are guaranteed in both the U.S. and individual state constitutions. Most rights of a free people emanate from private property rights. A strong case can be made that property owners do not own their property and only "rent" their land/ property. However, having more rights on your side while owning land will only help you long term.

Usually, it is not possible to stop the government from taking your property by eminent domain. Eminent Domain is the "right of a government or its agent to expropriate private property for public use, with payment of compensation".

The power of Eminent Domain is the legal right of the government; however, you can oppose the government's requests when they are not acting justly. You can also refuse their compensation offer to ensure you can receive your fair sum. You will definitely receive strong pushback if you stall or delay plans they have made for the land, especially if you are planning to outright refuse to sell your land.

Quick Tip: If you outright refuse to engage in negotiations, this is where the government will forcible apply all of their legal rights to ensure you sell your land. What can be helpful is to continue to engage in negotiations whether you plan on selling or not. This helps keep the government at bay and (legally) requires them to act justly; if not, your price can go up which may be more than they wish to pay, and you keep your land. Dragging out and extending negotiations will create some resentment, but can stall plans enough that the government and/or major companies/corporations may choose another location for plans they have.

You are entitled to compensation under Federal (and most state) Law regarding eminent domain. It is important to have an experienced Eminent Domain Attorney in your network when you own land. The reason you need an experienced eminent domain Attorney is to make sure you get maximum compensation and damages for your property or business.

A key point to consider is that Eminent Domain is not just the government confiscating land from a person or group of people. Eminent Domain is simply about protection (for whoever it applies to).

The Case of Bruce's Beach (Eminent Domain)

In Manhattan Beach, California, there's a beachfront property ("Bruce's Beach"), which was once a seaside resort, owned by Charles and Willa Bruce who were a Black couple that catered to those who identified as Black and/or African American during the Jim Crow era in the United States. The city of Manhattan Beach claimed the property in 1924 through eminent domain and vastly underpaid the Bruce's for their land. This resort was a prime location for vacation for those underserved and subject to overt and covert racism in the United States.

Migrating from New Mexico in the early 20th century, Willa and Charles Bruce were among the first Black people to settle into what would become Manhattan Beach, California. In 1912, purchased two parcels of land on Highland Avenue for less than $2,000 and built a beachfront lodge with a café, dance hall, cabanas, and bathing suit rentals. This lodge is considered to be the first Black-Owned resort on the West Coast which opened during a time where Jim Crow Laws barred Black people from seashores.

"Wherever I tried to buy land for a beach resort, we have been refused" Willa Bruce told the Los Angeles Times in 1912. "But I own this land and I am going to keep it". The Bruce's were able to purchase the property because prominent real estate developer George Peck chose to ignore segregation policies in the area and sold land to many other African Americans, allowing several thriving Black American communities to thrive around California.

Willa handled most of the lodge business as Charles was often out of town working as a railroad dining car chef. Almost immediately upon opening, guests were harassed by white neighbors and members of the Ku Klux Klan, who reportedly slashed the guests' tires and set fire to mattress under the main building. Furthermore, fake "10-minute only" parking signs were posted to reduce visitors from out of town. Finally, in 1924, the Manhattan Beach City Council used eminent domain to condemn the Bruce's' Lodge, along with several other nearby Black-owned properties and claimed the land.

Since, the land has remained relatively untouched and preserved. After a long-fought battle, the land that was taken via eminent domain, has been returned to its' rightful owners. During Jim Crow, this land could have been seized and/or destroyed, making the land have little to not value. But, due to the land being taken by eminent domain (although unjustly), the owners of this land were able to return the land back to its rightful owners without alterations or contingencies. If not taken by eminent domain, this land could be owned by several different owners, which would make getting this land back almost impossible.

The story of the Bruce family should be taken as a lesson on thinking long-term when investing in land, but also remaining knowledgeable of particular rights and laws such as eminent domain. The Eminent Domain protection laws that were used to take their land, were the same laws used in court to return this very same land back to its rightful owners.

Today (2021) the average home in Manhattan Beach, California has a value of about $2,923,949. The land ("Bruce's Beach") being returned to the descendants of the Bruce family is estimated to have a value of $75,000,000.

Outline For Land Acquisition

Land acquisition is a process by which the government (state or union) can acquire private land for the purpose of infrastructure development, urbanization, or industrialization. In return, the government will pay a suitable compensation to the current landowner, as per the market value and would be responsible for the rehabilitation and resettlement of the affected landowners.

Since land is a scarce resource in a populated country like India, their government has formulated certain provisions, rules, and guidelines, to facilitate infrastructure development in areas where the land is privately owned, or being used for agricultural purposes. Known as the Right to Fair Compensation and Transparency in Land Acquisition, Rehabilitation and Resettlement Act, 2013, this law replaced the archaic Land Acquisition Act, 1894, to bring in a new procedure, which would grant fair compensation to those affected. As of today (2021) majority of land ownership can occur through purchasing outright. As land gets harder to purchase, countries are likely to move closer to applying Land Acquisition Laws to take land away from owners.

Land being scarce in countries like India, it is only a matter of time before other countries have to confront a similar issue and most likely, come up with their own form of Land Acquisition Laws which are outlined below.

Aims and objectives of the Land Acquisition Act, 2013

- To ensure a transparent process for acquiring land, in consultation with all the stakeholders and local governing bodies.
- To ensure minimum displacement of the existing population, owning or staying on the land.
- To provide fair compensation to the families who are affected or whose land has been acquired or livelihood has been affected, because of the land acquisition.
- To provide adequate provision for rehabilitation and resettlement of the families affected.

Provisions and Purpose of Land Acquisition

As per the Act, the government of India (state, as well as central) can procure land for its own use or for public sector companies or for 'public purpose', which can include any of these:

- For any work related to state or national security or defense services of India, which includes naval, military, air force or other armed forces, under the purview of the state or central government.
- For building public infrastructure but excluding private hospitals, private educational institutional and private hotels.

- For any project involving agriculture or allied industries, such as dairy, fisheries or meat processing, owned by the government or by farmer's cooperatives.
- For industrial corridors, manufacturing zones or other projects listed in the National Manufacturing Policy. This can also include mining activities.
- For water harvesting, conservation structure projects or for planned development or improvement of village sites.
- For government-aided educational and research institutions.
- For planned development, such as creating housing projects for the weaker sections, in rural or urban areas.
- For developing residential projects for the poor or landless, or for people affected by natural calamities.

Current Land Acquisition Act Timeline (India)

September 7, 2011: Land Acquisition, Rehabilitation and Resettlement Bill, 2011, introduced in the Lok Sabha.

August 29, 2013: Bill passed in the Lok Sabha.

September 4, 2013: Bill passed in the Rajya Sabha.

September 27, 2013: Bill receives the president's approval.

January 1, 2014: Land Acquisition Act comes into force.

May 30, 2015: President promulgates the amendment.

In the outline below you will view the detailed process of Land Acquisition (which should make its way into other countries on a more individual level in the near future).

Land acquisition is normally done in three ways:

1. Acquisition under Right to Fair Compensation and Transparency in Land Acquisition, Rehabilitation and Resettlement Act, 2013 (LARR ACT, 2013).

2. Private negotiations with the landowners.
3. Acquisition through other Acts.

1. Acquisition under Right to Fair Compensation and Transparency in Land Acquisition, Rehabilitation and Resettlement Act, 2013

- The Right to Fair Compensation and Transparency in Land Acquisition, Rehabilitation and Resettlement Act, 2013 ("LARR Act") came into force after repealing the Land Acquisition Act, 1894. Under this Act, the District Collector facilitates the process of land acquisition when the acquisition is done for public purpose. Through this Act, the Developer is able to acquire land after complying with the provisions under this Act.

The land acquisition process as under the 2013 Act is as follows:

- A Social Impact Assessment study (SIA) is to be prepared by the project proponent (developer) under section 4. It is to be done in consultation (involving a public hearing with locals) with the concerned Panchayat, municipality, or Municipal Corporation under section 5 outlining:

    1. Whether the acquisition will serve the public purpose,
    2. The estimation of how many families will be affected,
    3. The number of families which may have to be displaced,
    4. Other common properties which may be affected in their area,
    5. Whether any other alternative place has been considered by the government,
    6. The overall cost of the project and the benefit of the project.

- An expert group under section 7 approves the social impact assessment (SIA) report and makes recommendations within

2 months about whether the project can go ahead or should be abandoned and also give the reasons for their decision.

- Examination and approval of proposals for land acquisition and the social impact assessment report is done by the state government under Section 8 to determine whether the land is needed for any public purpose.

- After the approval, as per section 11 of the Act whenever a land in any area is required or likely to be required for any public purpose, a public notification along with details of the land is to be published in the official gazette and 2 daily local newspapers in that locality. This is the initial acquisition notice.

- A time period of 60 days is given for the general public to raise objections before the collector under Section 15.

- Preliminary land survey reports are prepared under Section 12.

- The Rehabilitation and Resettlement (R&R) report is prepared by the Administrator, Rehabilitation and Resettlement under section 16 and after review by the collector, made public under Section 18.

- There is a publication of the declaration of the acquisition under Section 19 with a summary of the rehabilitation and resettlement scheme.

- The land is marked, measured, and planned by the collector and project proponent under Section 20 unless already done under Section 12.

- Final notice under Section 21 is given to the persons interested to make any claims to compensations and rehabilitation and resettlement about the acquisition before the Collector within a period of 60 days.

- Land acquisition award is made by the collector under Section 23 to persons claiming compensation and rehabilitation and resettlement after enquiry.

- Possession of land shall be taken by the Collector under Section 38.

    - o It is pertinent to note that no consent is required for acquisitions for government projects, Consent of 70% of landowners required for the acquisition of land with respect to Public-Private Partnership projects and Consent of 80% landowners required for land acquisition for private projects.
    - o Anticipated timeline for land acquisition as per land is somewhere around 500 days. In addition to the entire process, there are several other clearances and approvals required for real estate projects to commence construction.

2 Acquisition Through Direct Negotiations With Landowners

- Direct private negotiations with landowners for acquiring land are permitted under the LARR Act, 2013. These can be resorted to so the land can be acquired without adhering to the long procedure under the LARR Act, 2013 or a small patch of land is left inadvertently during initial acquisition.

- It involves the constitution of a negotiation committee by the state government having the district collector as part of it. The compensation and multiplying factor are as per the State Government rules.

- An example of when this was done can be seen when the Maharashtra government, in 2015, decided to acquire land for new non-irrigation projects through negotiations by having a 7-member committee headed by the district collector for deciding the compensation payable to the landowner.

The steps are as follows:

1. A negotiation committee is constituted by the State Govt.
2. Joint inspection is done of the alignment of requirements with all concerned departments & landowners.
3. Negotiations with landowners are undertaken for fixing rates of the land.
4. Recommendations by the committee and their approval by State Govt.
5. Award by the Collector, payment is made, and possession of Land is transferred.

3. Acquisition Through Other Acts

The LARR Act, 2013 has exempted acts as National Highways Act, 1956 and the Railways Act, 1989 from its purview. The acquisition under these Acts can be done as per the provisions in the respective acts although the compensation, rehabilitation and resettlement provisions of these acts have to be in consonance with the provisions under LARR Act, 2013.

The Land Title Verification Process

- The title verification is done to trace the history of ownership of the land up to the last thirty years to determine whether the title is marketable and good.

- The procedure outlined below lays down the considerations that need to be made when the title of land is being verified. The following steps are undertaken when a title verification is conducted:

    - The **owner of the property and the area needs to be ascertained** by using the survey number of the land. A lot of states have digitized land records but if that hasn't happened in a state, the land records can be accessed at the office of the sub-registrar by making an application prescribed although RTIs are the preferred mode of obtaining information. (In Maharashtra, this can be done by accessing this online resource: https://mahabhunakasha.mahabhumi.gov.in/27/index.jsp)

- The next step will be extracting primary documents to ascertain the ownership of the land.

The documents needed shall be:

1. Record of Rights (7/12 extract, satbarautara); and
2. Register of mutation (form VI).

The above mentioned land records are maintained at the office of the sub-registrar and an RTI can be made to receive these records.

Alternatively, due to the digitization of land records, information can be available online. (For example, in Maharashtra https://bhulekh.mahabhumi.gov.in/ can be accessed to view the 7/12 extract and Form VIIIA provided the district/taluka is known.)

If an issue is faced in finding the survey number required, the same can be received by making an RTI application with the Land Records department.

The **following documents should be analyzed and examined** to ascertain:

- o The ownership, land share, encumbrances, pending land disputes, occupancy rights.
- o Details of transactions the land has been part of including price of land as paid by current owner provided account number as mentioned.
- o Details of legal heirs of deceased owners of property.
- o Total land holding of the owner in specific land.
- o Details of change in title of property.

- o Possession can be investigated by visiting the land. It is crucial to ensure that a person who is the owner on the document also exercises the actual control over the land.
- o Type of land- agricultural/non-agricultural.
- o Easement Rights, if granted to any other person.

Search should be done at the office of Sub Registrar for additional documents:

1. Reconciliation should be done with book no 1, Index no 1 and 2 maintained with the sub registrar to check for non-testamentary documents, names of parties to every registered transaction and particulars of property that is the subject matter of a registered transaction respectively. (can be accessed by making application to sub registrar)
2. Encumbrance Certificate certifying piece of land free from encumbrances. (Form XVI) [N/A in certain states like Maharashtra]

- **Release certificate** can be requested from banks if traceable liability is reflected in 7/12 extract against a bank.
- The **Power of Attorney** of agents selling land should be verified (should be registered as well) and the land dealt with in the Power of Attorney should be checked as well.
- **Additional searches** can be made with the Registrar of Companies, the Courts to check for litigations and the Central Registry of Securitization Assets Reconstruction and Security Interest (CERSAI) to check for loans.
- In the title report prepared subsequently, all the aforementioned points of investigation should be clearly mentioned.

- After the title is verified as good and marketable, the land acquisition process should be initiated.

Conclusion

Any lapses in title verification or the acquisition process can keep the land required for the project tied up in litigation and disputes leading to a delay in completion of the project and huge monetary losses. Therefore, it is essential to follow the steps in verifying the land title and in the subsequent acquisition as mentioned above (considering the differences that may need to be factored in due to different rules in different states) to ensure the start of the project is hassle-free and all the other approvals and clearances can be received.

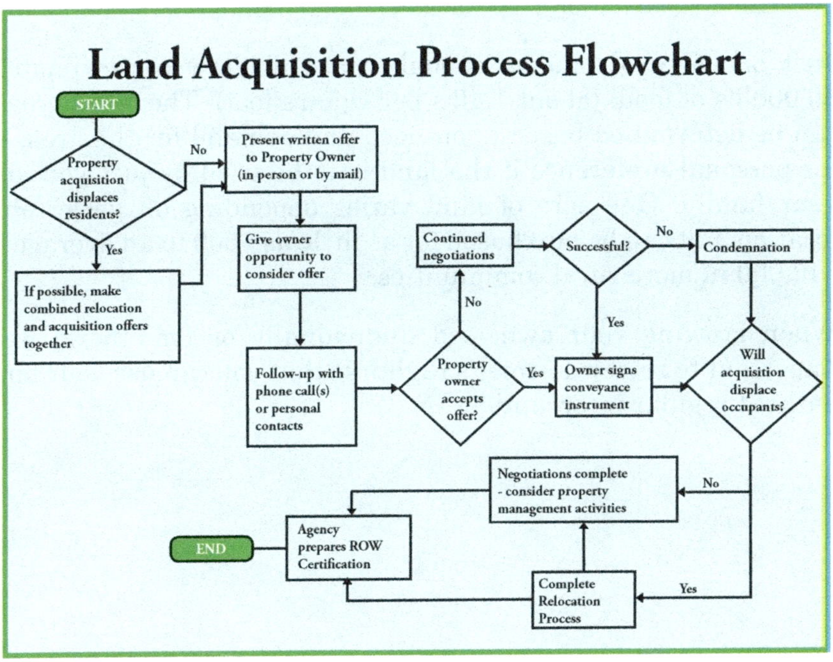

As stated earlier, land is being purchased quickly for development, while no land can be added to the planet. Upon purchasing land today, this may prepare you for future compensation or negotiations via Land Acquisition from your local or state government (or private property). You may wish to not sell your land even if presented with a large offer. Preserving land is necessary and is not only conducted through the government; we as individuals can contribute to this as well.

As we remain uncertain of what the world may look like, we must plan accordingly for the world we want to create. Many of us may purchase land and remain uncertain of what to do with it or plans to create. Others many move forward with a well-established plan for what they are going to use the land for. We can use these opportunities to come together and establish ways to use the many systems in place to our own benefit towards self-sustainability. To go along with the premise of this book, using land to grow produce is, and will always be a necessity, whether we own the land, or the government, or major corporations.

Just one acre of land is enough space to grow approximately 60,000lbs of food! (about 1.4lbs per square foot). The foods grown can be determined based upon need and demand for the area, or for personal preference if the land is to be used by just you and your family. One acre of land varies depending on geographic location, but can be purchased for as little as $500 to an average of $12,000 in more rural communities.

When growing your own food (individually or for others) it is important to review Farmer's Rights so that you can use your land without regular interruption.

10 Farmer 's Rights

After you have purchased land, you want to be familiar with Rights the go along with your plans. Creating a growing space would mean you are protected by Farmer's Rights. You do not need to grow and sell produce in order to be protected by Farmer's Rights; nor do you have to fulfill the obligation of being a "Farmer". If you own land in which you grow your own foods, you are protected by Farmer's Rights.

These Right's consist of the rights of Farmers to save, use, exchange and sell farm-saved seed and propagating material, their rights to be recognized, rewarded, and supported for their contribution to the global pool of genetic resources as well as to the development of commercial varieties of plants, and to participate in decision making on issues related to crop genetic resources.

Brief History of Farmer's Rights

In the early 1980's, the idea of "Farmer's Rights" came about after the increased demand for "Plant Breeder's Rights". Farmer's Rights gained momentum as they worked to draw attention to the view that Farmers were the foundation for all plant breeding and should have rights before the Plant Breeders. Main topics of discussion that were covered in defense of the Farmers were, informal consultations on plant genetic resources and the Keystone Dialogue; initiatives that connected the global seafood business to science, connected fishermen to aquaculture, and connected European and American companies to Asian companies.

In 1989, Farmer's Rights were first established by the FAO (Food And Agricultural Organization) Conference, and in 1991 the FAO Conference created a fund for the realization of these rights. As a result of the support for Farmer's Rights by the FAO, the FAO was urged that ways and means be explored to develop complementarity and cooperation between the Convention of

Biological Diversity (CBD) and the work of the FAO on plant genetic resources for food and agriculture. Particularly, the FAO was urged to seek solutions to outstanding matters, including Farmer's Rights. This marked the start of lengthy negotiations which finally led to the International Treaty. The International Treaty is a comprehensive international agreement that aims to guaranteeing food security through the conservation, exchange, and sustainable use of the world's plant genetic resources for food and agriculture, the fair and equitable benefit of sharing arising from its use, and the recognition of Farmer's Rights.

In 1996, the Global Plan for the Conservation and Sustainable Utilization of Plant Genetic Resources for Food and Agriculture was adopted by the International Technical Conference on Plant Genetic resources. It too, advocated for the issue of Farmer's Rights. With the adoption of the International Treaty in 2001, a legally binding international agreement was established for the management of plant genetic resources for food and agriculture, in which states are obliged to protect and promote Farmer's Rights.

Foundation of Farmer's Rights

- Reward To Farmer's: the enormous collective contribution of past, present, and future farmers to the global genetic pool had to be recognized in practical terms. The rights holders would not be individuals, but entire groups of peoples. Measures such as freer exchange of plant genetic resources, sharing of information and research results, and training are covered here. Benefit sharing was an important aspect of the discussion, but interpretations varied. Some suggested benefit sharing on a bilateral basis, whereas others argues that such a system would not be feasible due to the nature of exchange of agricultural resources over time; it would not be possible to detect countries or origin, and the transaction costs would be too high. Therefore, a multilateral system was suggested which came in the form of the *International Treaty.*
- Balancing Breeder's Rights: the concept emerged from the debate on intellectual property rights to plant genetic

resources. Initially, the major concerns were how to ensure that such rights would not be detrimental to the customary practices of farmers to save, reuse, share, and develop plant varieties. These practices were seen as the basis for their continued contribution to conservation and innovation in genetic resources, and should therefore be protected. Farmer's rights were viewed as a means towards this end.

- Conservation Of Plant Genetic Resources and Related Knowledge: Balancing Breeder's rights was one way to ensure that farmers were not hindered in maintaining their customary practices. However, more direct measure would be required to enable farmers to continue to act as custodians of the plant genetic heritage and as innovators in agriculture. Measures to conserve plant genetic resources and related knowledge and to stimulate innovations were therefore seen as essential. These measures were sometimes addressed in the context of rewards and benefit sharing. However, they were also deemed important as an independent component of Farmer's Rights, vital to present and future food security.
- International Fund: all parties agreed to establish an international fund for Farmer's Rights which would provide the necessary resources needed to reward and support farmers for their continued contributions to the conservation and development of plant genetic resources for food and agriculture.

These principal stand as the foundations of Farmer's Rights. They represent the long and complex negotiations that took place, and need to be taken into consideration when implementing the International Treaty at the national as well as the multilateral level.

Farmer's Rights

1. Right 1L Access To Seed [Section 39(1)(iv)]
2. Right 2: Benefit Sharing [Section 26]
3. Right 3: Compensation [Section 39(2)]

4. Right 4: Reasonable Seed Price [Section 47]
5. Right 5: Farmers' Recognition and reward For Contributing To Conservation [Section 39(i)(iii) & Section 45(2)(C)]
6. Right 6: Registration of Farmer's Varieties [Section 39(1)(iii)]
7. Right 7: Prior Authorization For The Commercialization of Essentially Derived Varieties [Section 28 (6)]
8. Right 8: Exemption From Registration Fees For Farmer's [Section 44]
9. Right 9: Farmer Protection From Innocent Infringement [Section 42]

Right 1: Access to seed [Section 39(1)(iv)]

Farmers are entitled to save, use, sow, re-sow, exchange, share or sell their farm produce, including seed of protected varieties, in the same manner as they were entitled to before the coming into force to the PPV&FR Act. However, farmers are not entitled to sell branded seed of a variety protected under this Act. Farmers can use farm saved seed from a crop cultivated in their own.

Right 2: Benefit sharing [Section 26]

Plant breeders and legal entities including farmers who provide Plant Genetic Resources (PGR) to breeders for developing new varieties shall receive a fair share of benefit from the commercial gains of the registered varieties. Out of all the national plant variety protection laws enacted since 2001, the PPV&FR Act is the first that integrates a provision for access and benefit-sharing (ABS) along with Plant Breeder's Rights (PBRs). Accession of the genetic resource used in breeding is permitted under the Biological Diversity Act, 2002. However, the PPV&FR Act requires a breeder to make a sworn declaration on the geographical origin of the genetic resources used in the pedigree of the new variety, and its accession.

Right 3: Compensation [Section 39(2)]

Registered seed must be sold with the full disclosure of their agronomic performance under recommended management conditions. When such seed is sold to farmers but fails to provide the expected performance under recommended management conditions, the farmer is eligible to claim compensation from the breeder through the intervention of the PPV&FR Authority.

Right 4: Reasonable seed price [Section 47]

Farmers have the right to access seed of registered varieties at a reasonable and remunerative price. When this condition is not met, the breeder's exclusive right over the variety is suspended under the provision concerning compulsory licensing, and the breeder is obligated to license the seed production, distribution, and sales of the variety to a competent legal entity. Most of the laws for plant variety protection have provisions on compulsory licensing of protected varieties to ensure adequate seed supply to farmers, and several of them also use unfair pricing as grounds for compulsory licensing.

Right 5: Farmers' recognition and reward for contributing to conservation [Section 39(i)(iii) & Section 45(2)(C)]

Farmers who have been engaged in PGR conservation and crop improvement, and who have made substantial contributions in providing genetic resources for crop improvement, receive recognition and rewards from the national gene fund. The gene fund receives resources from the implementation of the Act, which in turn are complemented by contribution from national and international organizations. The expenditures of the fund are earmarked to support the conservation and sustainable use of PGR, and in this way, it can be considered to be a national equivalent to the global benefit-sharing fund operating within the International Treaty on Plant Genetic Resources for Food and Agriculture.

Since 2007, the Plant Genome Saviour/Community awards, associated with the national gene fund, has been rewarding farming communities and individual farmers for their contribution to in-situ and on farm conservation to the selection of PGR.

The Authority in consultation with Government of India, has established five Plant Genome Saviour Community Awards of Rs 10 Lakh each along with citation and memento to be conferred every year to the farming communities for their contribution in the conservation of Plant Genetic Resources.

In accordance with the Protection of Plant Varieties and Farmers' Rights (Recognition and Rewards from the Gene Fund) Rules, 2010 the Authority also setup ten Plant Genome Saviour Farmer Reward of Rs 1 Lakh each with citation & memento and also twenty Plant Genome Saviour Farmer Recognition annually from 2012-13 to the farmers engaged in the conservation of the Genetic Resources of the landraces and wild relatives of economics plants and their improvement through selection and preservation.

Right 6: Registration of farmers' varieties [Section 39(1) (iii)]

The PPV&FR Act allows for the registration of existing farmers' varieties that fulfill requirements for distinctness, uniformity, stability, and denomination, but does not include that of novelty. This right provides farmers with a one-off opportunity for a limited period of time, from the moment when a crop species is species is included in the crop portfolio under the PPV&FR Act for registration. Once registered, these varieties are entitled to all PBRs.

Right 7: Prior authorization for the commercialization of essentially derived varieties [Section 28 (6)]

When farmers' varieties, whether extant or new, are used by a third party as source material for the development of an essentially derived variety, the farmers need to provide prior authorization for its commercialization. Such a process can allow farmers to negotiate the terms of authorization with the breeder, which may include royalties, benefit-sharing, etc.

Right 8: Exemption from registration fees for farmers [Section 44]

Under PPV&FR Act, farmers have the privilege of being completely exempted from payment of any kind of fees or other payments that are normally payable for variety registration; tests for distinctness, uniformity, and stability (DUS), and other services rendered by the PPV&FR Authority; as well as for legal proceedings related to infringement or other causes in courts, tribunal, etc.

Right 9: Farmer protection from innocent infringement [Section 42]

If a farmer can prove before court that he or she was not aware of the existence of any rights at the time of an infringement on any such rights, as detailed in the PPV&FR Act, he or she will not be charged. This provision is made in consideration of the centuries-old unrestrained rights that the farmers had over the seed of all varieties, the novel nature of the PPV&FR Act and the poor legal literacy of farmers

Farmer's Rights In India (Land Acquisition Country)

1. Right 1: Right To Seed
2. Right 2: Right To Register Varieties
3. Right 3: Right To Reward and Recognition
4. Right 4: Right To Benefit Sharing
5. Right 5: Right To Information and Compensation For Crop Failure
6. Right 6: Right To Compensation For Undisclosed Use Of Traditional varieties
7. Right 7: Right To Adequate Availability of Registered material

Right 1: Rights to Seed

The farmer's right to save and exchange seed has been one of the major demands of the farmers' right movement. India's Act aims to give farmers the right to save, use, exchange or sell seed in the same manner he/she was entitled to before the Act. However, the right to sell seed is restricted in that the farmer cannot sell seed in a packaged form labelled with the registered name

Right 2: Right to Register Varieties

Farmers like commercial breeders can apply for IPR over their varieties. The criterion for registration of varieties is also similar to breeders (distinctness, uniformity, stability) but novelty is not a requirement. The ability to gain IPR type rights over farmers' varieties is a unique aspect of India's law. Farmers' variety is defined as 'a variety which has been traditionally cultivated and evolved by farmers in their fields; or is a wild relative or landrace of a variety about which the farmers possess common knowledge'. The plant breeder's right granted on farmers' varieties provides the exclusive right to produce and market the seed of registered varieties (Bala Ravi, 2004).

Right 3: Right to Reward and Recognition

The Act provides for establishing a National Gene Fund. Through the National Gene Fund, farmers that have played a role in conservation of varietal development of plants can be recognized and rewarded. The fee collected from breeders who are required to pay for benefit sharing is to be deposited in the National Gene Fund. The money collected under the National Gene Fund can be used for support and reward farmers engaged in conservation. The Act provides this general provision to promote conservation but does not provide further specifications regarding the method. The Authority set up under the Act is left with the task of operationalizing this right.

Right 4: Right to Benefit Sharing

The Act proposes the setting up of a centralized National Gene Fund through which benefit sharing would be facilitated. The Authority is required to publish the registered varieties and invite claims for benefit sharing. The Act states that any person or group of persons or firm or governmental or nongovernmental organization can submit its claim of benefit sharing. The rewards from the gene fund can only be given to a farmer/community who can prove that they have contributed to the selection and preservation of materials used in the registered variety (Mauria, 2004).

Right 5: Right to Information and Compensation for Crop Failure

Section 39 (2) of the Act provides that the breeder must give information about expected performance of the registered variety. If the material fails to perform, the farmers may claim for compensation under the Act. This provision attempts to ensure that seed companies do not make exaggerated claims about the performance (yield, pest resistance) to the farmer. It enables farmers to apply to the Authority for compensation in case they suffer losses due to the failure of the variety to meet the targets claimed by the companies.

Right 6: Right to Compensation for Undisclosed use of Traditional Varieties

In cases where it is established that the breeder has not disclosed the source of varieties belonging to a particular community, compensation can be granted through the Gene Fund. Any NGO, individual or government institution may file a claim for compensation on behalf of the local community in cases where the breeder has not disclosed traditional knowledge or resources of the community.

Right 7: Right to Adequate Availability of Registered Material

The breeder is required to provide adequate supply of seeds or material of the variety to the public at a reasonable price. If after three years of registration of the variety, the breeder fails to do so, any person can apply to the Authority for a compulsory license. Compulsory licenses revoke the exclusive right given to the breeder and enable third parties to produce, distribute or sell the registered variety. Right to Free Services: The Act exempts farmers from paying fees for registration of a variety, for conducting tests on varieties, for renewal of registration, for opposition and for fees on all legal proceedings under the Act. (Bala Ravi, 2004) Protection from legal infringement in case of lack of awareness: Considering low literacy levels in the country, the Act provides safeguards against innocent infringement by farmers. Farmers who unknowingly violate the rights of a breeder shall not be punished if he/she can prove that they were not aware of the existence of breeder's rights.

11 Helpful Resources

Gardening Websites

- Gardener's Supply Company: Here are some helpful tips for first-timers, including the best type of plants for beginners and how to time your efforts to maximize your transplanting success.

  https://www.gardeners.com/how-to/how-to-start-seeds/5062.html

- Mother Earth News: Check out these tips about which seed starting mix and containers to use and why, how much light and heat to give your seeds and what to expect from your seedlings as they progress.

  https://www.motherearthnews.com/organic-gardening/gardening-techniques/starting-seeds-indoors-zm0z12djzsor

- New York Botanical Garden (video): Follow along as Sonia Uyterhoeven from the New York Botanical Garden shows you how to start seeds indoors.

  https://www.youtube.com/watch?v=thGois-BqHY

- Smart Gardener: This online garden planner is a great resource to map out your garden. Their database of 3,000 organic, non-GMO plants will help you decide what to grow, plot out how much space you need to alot for the plants you've chosen and make a helpful garden to-do list and schedule.

  https://www.smartgardener.com/

- American Horticultural Society Gardening Resources: If you are looking for more books, tips, or information, this list of gardening resources from the American Horticultural Society (the experts when it comes to gardening) has you covered. They also have tons of information in The American Gardener, a bi-monthly magazine that covers a variety of gardening topics.

https://ahsgardening.org/gardening-resources/

- Farmers' Almanac: A classic farming handbook, the website edition of the almanac has a U.S. Plant Hardiness Zone Map, which can help determining which plants are suitable for which areas as well as a gardening calendar with dates to do certain tasks by.

  https://www.farmersalmanac.com/home-garden

- National Gardening Association: If you are looking for my educational resources, the National Gardening Association has online gardening courses along with robust guides for gardening a variety of fruits and vegetables.

  https://garden.org/

- Cornell University Garden Based Learning: These educational resources from Cornell University are garden-based activities that can be used for a short- or longer-term project. designed to target ages 6-14, although they are adaptable for other ages.

  https://gardening.cals.cornell.edu/

Gardening Books

- The Garden Primer by Barbara Damrosch: This classic gardening book with an emphasis on sustainable methods is a user-friendly gardening encyclopedia jam-packed with gardening facts, helpful hints, landscape design advice, tips on gardening gear, how to buy plants and specifics for individual plants.

- The Vegetable Gardener's Bible by Edward C. Smith: Now in its 10th edition, Ed Smith created the W-O-R-D system, otherwise known as wide rows, organic methods, raised beds and deep soil, making his book essential reading for organic gardeners everywhere.

- All New Square Foot Gardening II: The Revolutionary Way to Grow More in Less Space by Mel Bartholomew: Author and gardening innovator Mel Bartholomew developed his techniques for small space gardening in the 1980s, leading his book to sell more than two million copies. His second edition includes tips for vertical gardening, meaning you can make even more use of your space.
- Rodale's Ultimate Encyclopedia of Organic Gardening by Fern Marshall Bradley: This comprehensive resource from Rodale covers both gardening and landscaping information including garden design, pest control, organic soil practices, edible landscaping, community gardening, stone scaping, and earth-friendly techniques for gardening in a changing climate.
- Carrots Love Tomatoes: Secrets of Companion Planting for Successful Gardening by Louise Riotte: Originally published in 1975, this is the book gardeners grab when they prefer pest-resistant planning to using chemicals. The practical books suggest what plants grow best together, which herbals sprays can help controls insects and which wild plants are good to encourage.

How To Build A Garden Bed:

Scan QR Code or follow the link below.
https://homesteadandchill.com/how-to-build-raised-garden-bed/

Testing Soil:

Scan QR Code(s) or follow each link below.
http://www.washingtonyouthgarden.org/washingtonyouthgarden/soil-test-tips-7-simple-steps

Video
https://www.youtube.com/watch?v=CtzpYraKNkc

Transplanting:

Scan QR Code(s) or follow each link below.
https://www.youtube.com/watch?v=oq2ReaUz19k
https://www.plantedwell.com/gardening-websites-blogs/

References

1. https://prsindia.org/billtrack/the-right-to-fair-compensation-and-transparency-in-land-acquisition-rehabilitation-and-resettlement-second-amendment-bill-2015
2. https://www.business-standard.com/article/economy-policy/maharashtra-govt-decides-to-acquire-land-through-negotiations-115051300027_1.html
3. https://legislative.gov.in/sites/default/files/A2013-30.pdf
4. http://ficci.in/spdocument/20140/real-estate.pdf
5. https://slidetodoc.com/land-acquisition-land-acquisition-options-1-land-acquisition-2/
6. https://prsindia.org/billtrack/the-right-to-fair-compensation-and-transparency-in-land-acquisition-rehabilitation-and-resettlement-amendment-bill-2015
7. https://rightsandresources.org/wp-content/uploads/2016/11/Land-Disputes-and-Stalled-Investments-in-India_November-2016.pdf
8. https://www.livemint.com/industry/manufacturing/-63-billion-of-stalled-residential-projects-in-india-sound-warning-for-banks-11570168016947.html
9. https://soilsmatter.wordpress.com/2017/05/15/what-can-i-tell-by-looking-at-and-touching-my-soil/
10. https://www.soils4teachers.org/files/s4t/texture.pdf
11. https://homesteadandchill.com/how-to-build-raised-garden-bed/

12. https://www.nrcs.usda.gov/wps/portal/nrcs/detail/soils/edu/?cid=nrcs142p2_054311

13. https://www.soils.org/about-soils/contaminants/

14. https://hgic.clemson.edu/factsheet/soil-texture-analysis-the-jar-test/

15. https://www.trees.com/gardening-and-landscaping/free-garden-planners

16. https://organismalbio.biosci.gatech.edu/growth-and-reproduction/plant-development-i-tissue-differentiation-and-function/

17. https://www.investopedia.com/terms/z/zoning.asp

18. https://www.massaudubon.org/our-conservation-work/policy-advocacy/shaping-climate-resilient-communities/publications-community-resources/guidebook-to-involvement-in-your-community/chapter-4-zoning-regulatory-land-use-controls-incentives

19. https://greenlaw.blogs.pace.edu/2014/11/03/using-zoning-to-protect-the-environment-an-excerpt-from-protecting-the-environment-through-land-use-law-standing-ground/

20. https://www.farmersalmanac.com/a-tree-that-owns-itself-25869

21. https://ap.fftc.org.tw/article/600

22. https://vikaspedia.in/agriculture/policies-and-schemes/crops-related/protection-of-plant-varieties-and-rights-of-farmers/farmers2019-rights-in-the-ppv-fr-act-2001

23. https://www.plantauthority.gov.in/

24. https://www.gardeners.com/how-to/how-to-start-seeds/5062.html

25. https://www.motherearthnews.com/organic-gardening/gardening-techniques/starting-seeds-indoors-zm0z12djzsor

26. https://www.youtube.com/watch?v=thGois-BqHY

27. https://www.smartgardener.com/

28. https://ahsgardening.org/gardening-resources/

29. https://www.farmersalmanac.com/home-garden

30. https://garden.org/

31. https://gardening.cals.cornell.edu/

Other Works By Author:

Available on Amazon

https://www.amazon.com/s?i=stripbooks&rh=p_27%3ABryan+Mcaskill&s=relevancerank&text=Bryan+Mcaskill&ref=dp_byline_sr_book_1

(Fasting) Also Available on Balboa Press

https://www.balboapress.com/en/bookstore/bookdetails/820758-fasting

Make Sure To Stay Connected By Following On *Social Media!*

Instagram:

@bryan_mcaskill

https://instagram.com/bryan_mcaskill?utm_medium=copy_link

@herbal.healing781

https://instagram.com/herbal.healing781?utm_medium=copy_link

Facebook:

Herbal Healing by Bryan McAskill

https://www.facebook.com/herbal.healing781/

HERBAL HEALING

by Bryan McAskill

Thank you **for your purchase and for reading this book.**

Hope you've enjoyed it!

Made in the USA
Monee, IL
03 November 2026

67385535R00085